Caribbean Publishing in Britain

A Tribute to Arif Ali

Asher & Martin Hoyles

WITHDRAWN

H
HANSIB

Published by Hansib Publications in 2011
London & Hertfordshire

Hansib Publications Limited
P.O. Box 226, Hertford, Hertfordshire, SG14 3WY, UK

Email: info@hansib-books.com
Website: www.hansib-books.com

A catalogue record for this book is
available from the British Library

ISBN: 978-1-906190-42-2

Production by Print Resources, Hertfordshire

Printed and bound in the UK

ACKNOWLEDGEMENTS

We would like to thank the following people for their invaluable help and encouragement in producing this book: Hakim Adi, Juliet Alexander, Kash Ali and Isha Persaud at Hansib, Sharon Atkin, Abiola Awojobi, Shango Baku, Caroline Bressey, Jan Carew, Sean Creighton, Navnit Dholakia, Shreela Flather, Jennifer Francis, Ros Howells, Rosa Hoyles, Christopher Johnson, Rory Lalwan, Herman Ouseley, Richard Painter, Alex Pascall, Shridath Ramphal, Earle Robinson, Jonathan Schneer, Clem Seecharan, Keith Vaz, Tony Wade, Ansel Wong, Simon Woolley.

Arif would also like to thank the many people who have helped him with his publishing and campaigning activities over the last 40 years. There are too many to mention them all, but they include the following: Aaron Cooper, Aaron Haynes, Abiola Awojobi, Adam Licudi, Adelaide Tambo, Akyaaba Addai-Sebo, Al Crosdale, Al Hamilton, Alan Cross, Alan Stinton, Alex Pascall, Alfonso Charles, Allan Aflak, Allison George, Allister Hennessey, Allister Hughes, Alvira Khan, Amela Vanderpool-Kubisch, Amina Hussein, Amos Ford, Angela Cox, Angela Whitter, Angie Benjamin, Angus Richmond, Angus Thompson, Ann Ramgoolie, Anon Saba Saakana, Ansel Wong, Anthony Wolfson, Arif Amin, Arlene Callendar, Arnold Dein, Arnon Adams, Arthur Dayfoot, Arthur France, Asher Hoyles, Ashton Gibson, Aziz Hadeed, Baldwin Spencer, Basdeo Panday, Basil Smith, B. B. Mitchell, Ben Bousquet, Bentley Roach, Beresford Edwards, Bernie Grant, Berry Edwards, Beverley Cooper, Bharrat Jagdeo, Bill Morris, Bill Jones, Bob Elliott, Bob Purkiss, Brendan Ali, Brenton Mitchell, Brian Belton, Brian Dyde, Brian Moyo, Bridgette Lawrence, Brinsley Samaroo, Buck Lopez, C. B. Patel, Cal James, Calvin Adams, Calvin James, Cameron Tudor, Candice Niles, Carl Abrams, Carl Budhan, Carmen Sloane, Carol Alfred, Caroline Bressey, Cassius Elias, Catherine Hogben, Caudley George, Cavendish Attwell, Cecil Pilgrim, Chandani Persaud, Charlotte Ali, Charles Maynard, Cheddi Jagan, Chris Hill, Chris Smith, Christopher Johnson, Claire Hynes, Clarence Thompson, Claude Brooks, Clem Seecharan, Clifford Robinson, Clive Lloyd, Colin Cumberbatch, Collin Carter, Courtney Laws, Dan Harriott, Dan Sweeney, Dan Thea, Danielle Elias, Darren Curtis, Dassi Govender, Dave Alcock, Dave Parrott, David Bookbinder, David Dabydeen, David Granger, David Johnson, David Mayberry, David Divine, David Matthews, Dave Beetlestone, David Pitt, David Roussel-Milner, David Shields, David Sparks, Dean Bailey, Deborah George, Deborah King, Derek San-Sellus, Devinia Sookia, Devon Gordon, Dhiren Basu, Divya Kohli, Donna Banks, Doreen Grey, Doris Harper, Drucilla Daley, Dudley Dryden, Dudley Thompson, Earl Luke, Earle Robinson, Eartha Springer, Ella Barnes, Elvis Donaldson, Emerson Braithwaite, Enyonam Afele, E. R. Braithwaite, Errol Barrow, Eslee Carberry, Esmund Bunsie, Essie Gardiner, Eugenia Charles, Eustace Guishard, Everton Forbes, Everton Forbes Jnr., Felix, Shareef Ali, Fermin Balado, Fidel Persaud, Flip Fraser, Forbes Burnham, Frank Birbalsingh, Frank Broome, Frank Crichlow, Frank David, Frank Thomasson, Gaia Goffe, Gale Henry, Garth Crooks, Gassel Gordon, George Berry, George Martin, George Senassy, Gilly Dee, Glen Jowitt, Gulam Meeran, Gulaam Noon, Gus John, Hakim Adi, Hal Austin, Harold Alleyne, Harold Lovell, Harry Levene, Hazel Smith, Hector Hanif Ali, Henderson Dalrymple, Herman Ouseley, Hermin Yorke, Horace Campbell, Howard Baugh, Hubert Charles, Hugh Marshall, Hugh Tinker, Humphrey Nemar, Hyacinth Moodie, Ian Marsh, Ian Mulder, Icelyn Grey, Ifeoma Onyefullu-Ebele, Iffat Aziz, Indul Kanhai, Iqbal Wahab, Irwin Douglas, Isabel Apio, Isha Persaud, Ivan Chin, Ivor Collins, J. A. Love, Jackie Hughes, Jackie Keizer, Jackie Vassal, Jacob Whittingham, Jacques Compton, Jah Bones, Jai Parasram, James Harrigan, James Hebblethwaite, James Hunte, James Rose, Jim Graham, Janet Lee-Walker, Janet Tappin, Janice Moore, J. C. Douglas, Jean Jones, Jeb Johnson, Jennifer Francis, Jenny Lawther, Janet Cooper, Jenny Pace, Jenny Rontganger, Jeremy Corbin, Jessica Bensley, Jim Yhap, Jimmy James, Jo Hall, Joan Applewhite, Joanna Reid, Joanne Hillhouse,

Joe Singh, Joe Whitter, Jonathan Schneer, John Benjamin, John Chapman, John Coleman, John Elva, John Hughes, John Singh, John St Lewis, John Thieme, Josephine Hazeley, Joyce Pascall, Joycelyn Barrow, Judith Goffe, Julie Roberts, Juliet Alexander, Junior Lincoln, Kamene Painter, Kamla Persad-Bissesar, Kamscilla Naidoo, Karen Twyman, Karen Woodberry, Kash Ali, Katherine Birbalsingh, Keith Bellott, Keith Bennett, Keith Sandiford, Keith Waite, Keith Vaz, Ken Campbell, Ken Drakett, Kendrick Chance, Kendrick Sooknarine, Kerry Thornton, Kenny Anthony, Kevin Le Gendre, Kevin Menhinick, Kevin Saul, Khalid Hassan, Kizzi Nkwocha, Kris Rampersad, Krishna Govender, Kuttan Menon, Laila Jabar-Coleman, Lascelles Poyser, Lateef Mathebula, Laurie Ince, Laurie Phillpotts, Lee Jasper, Lee Samuel, Leela Ramdin, Len Dyke, Len Jackman, Len Renwick, Leo Pennant, Lesley Hallett, Lester Bird, Lewis Cooper, Linda Haye, Lindsay Donald, Lionel Morrison, Liz Mackie, Lorna Clerice, Lubna Iqbal, Lucien Stephenson, Lucy Ali, Mairi Ali, Mamta Kapoor, Manny Cotter, Marc Wadsworth, Marcia Bullen, Marcia Manning, Mansukh Shah, Mario Bullen, Mark Christian,Mark Kamba, Mark Ponnampalm, Martin Hoyles, Marigold Saul, Mary Wilson, Maureen Lallgie, Maurice Bishop, Maurice Clarke, Mazrul Bacchus, Mervin Martin, Mia Morris, Michael Clerice, Michael Henry, Michael Hindley, Michael Martin, Michael Manley, Michael Mattus, Michael Williamson, Michel Maglorie, Michelle Wilson, Mike Branney, Ming Chan, Mirza Ahmad, Moti Persaud, Nadia Cattouse, Naqi Ali, Nana Wilson-Tagoe, Narend Sooknarine, Narendra Makanji, Navnit Dholakia, Nazmu Varani, Neema Kambona, Neil Kenlock, Neil Prendergast, Neil Shadbolt, Neil Wilson, Nikki Vounordis, Nimul Ali, Nisa Ali, Natalie Lopez, Nizam Ali, Nisa Khan, Noel Coobes, Norman Edwards, Oma Sawh, Omar Leon, Osborne Fleming, Ovid Holder, Owen Eversley, P. C. Southwell, Pamela Ali, Pamela Clark, Patrick Friday, Patrick Kodikara, Patsy Robertson, Paul Coleman, Paul Fraser, Paul Rich, Paul Reid, Paula Edgar, Pepe Francis, Petamber Persaud, Peter Kanhai, Peter Newson, Peter Paramananthum, Peter Ramrayka, Peter Tucker, Phil Sealy, Philip Straker, Phyllis Fleming-Banks, Prakash Singh, Praful Patel, Prasanna Probyn, Premindra Vaniak, Pushpinder Chowdhry, Rafina Rahaman-Rink, Rajandaye Ramkissoon-Chen, Rajiv Nair, Ralph Straker, Ralston Smith, Rawle Winston Titus, Raay Allan, Ray Goble, Reg Scarlett, Reginald Massey, Renee Webb, Reynold Francis, Rhoden Gordon, Richard Davis, Richard Painter, Ricky Christopher, Robert Birmingham, Robert Block, Robert Fernandez, Robert Govender, Robert McCoy, Rod Leon, Rod Westmass, Roderick Burrows, Rohan Kanhai, Rolando Vitale, Ronald Sanders, Ron Ramdin, Rory Lalwan, Ros Howells, Ross Slater, Roxanne Painter, Roy Adjodha, Roy Boyke, Roy Sawh, Rozan Hussein, Rudi Page, Rudy Narayan, Russell Lancaster, Russell Milner, Russell Pierre, Ruth Ansah Ayisis, Saba Saakanna, Sadhana Ghose, Sajid Ali, Salvatore Zuccarello, Sam Morris, Sam Selvarajah, Sam Ramgoolie, Sam Springer, Sammy Jay, Samuel Kennedy Yeboah, Sandra Record, Sara Govender, Sayrah Griffiths, Sean Creighton, Sebert Graham, Shango Baku, Shareef Ali, Sharmine Narayan, Sharon Atkin, Sharon Grant, Sharon White, Sharill Pink, Shawn Martin, Sheila Brown, Sheila Chin, Sherma McDougall, Shireen Bocas, Shirley Burgess, Shirley Hobson, Shreela Flather, Shridath Ramphal, Sibghat Kadri, Simon Augustine, Simon Lee, Simon Woolley, Sita Niland, Spartacus, Stefan Brazzo, Stephanie Dews, Stephen Broadbridge, Stephen Bulgin, Stephen Spencer, Steve Stephenson, Stewart Weathers, Sybil Phoenix, Tara Mukherjee, Tasadooq Ahmed, Tim England, Tim Sims, Tony Douglas, Tony George,Tony Matthews, Tony Wade, Trevor Carter, Trevor Lake, Tricia Reed, Tyrone Gopee, Victor Banks, Victor Crichlow, Victor Page, Victor Waldron, Vida Menzies, Vince Phillip, Vivien Brown, Walter Girling, Walter H. Roban, Wasim Raja, Wayne Francis, Wendy Ali, Wilfred Chen, Wilfred Wood, William Jones, William Trant, Winston McGowan, Winston Pickersgill, Wiseman Khuzwayo, Yasmin Narayan, Yasmin Painter, Yussuff Hanif, Yvonne Chew, Zahid Ali, Zahid Ally, Zeina Mason, Zerbanoo Gifford, Zoreen Ali, Zorena Yhap, Zuccarello Salvatore.

AUTHORS

Asher Hoyles is an additional support tutor, specialising in dyslexia, at NewVic Sixth Form College in Newham, east London. She is also a performance poet who runs performance poetry workshops.

Martin Hoyles taught in Newham secondary schools and at the University of East London. He has written books on gardening, childhood and literacy. His latest books are *The Axe Laid to the Root: The Story of Robert Wedderburn* and *Ira Aldridge: Celebrated 19th Century Actor.*

Together, Asher & Martin wrote *Remember Me: Achievements of Mixed Race People, Past and Present, Moving Voices: Black Performance Poetry* and *Dyslexia from a Cultural Perspective.*

Asher & Martin Hoyles, with their daughter Rosa

PREFACE

Our first meeting with Arif Ali was in 1998. We were trying to find a publisher for our book *Remember Me: Achievements of Mixed Race People, Past & Present.* The aim of the book was to provide our daughter Rosa, who was not yet three years old, with the background discussion on issues connected with being mixed race, so that when she grew older she would be able to determine for herself her own identity.

It seemed a simple concept to us, but persuading publishers of its significance was another matter! Although there was no book like it, they showed no interest. One publisher did ask us to discuss the idea and we had several meetings to decide who might be in the book. But when they suggested we include Mother Teresa, we realised that they had completely misunderstood what it was all about!

The last throw of the dice was to try Hansib. Then we realised that they should have been our first port of call. We received a letter and a phone call asking us to come and discuss the project.

So all three of us turned up at Fonthill Road in Finsbury Park, north London. We climbed the narrow stairs and found ourselves in an Aladdin's cave of an office. The walls were covered with posters and photos of all sorts of famous people and events and behind the big desk was the smiling figure of Arif. He greeted us all equally.

Rosa decided to wander round and explore, as she had recently learned to walk more confidently. Arif was happy to see her and offered her an orange and some crisps. It was clear that she had to be attended to first before we discussed business. This impressed us just as much as Arif's prompt acceptance of our manuscript. He clearly understood its aim and was very encouraging. The book was published the following year.

Asher, Martin & Rosa
September 2010

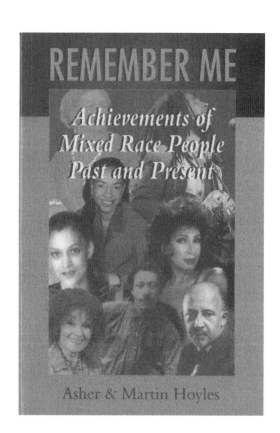

CONTENTS

Stokely Carmichael (Kwame Ture) with Arif in his office in Fonthill Road

Chapter 1

Introduction: Black Publishing in Britain

"We have a history, we don't know it, and we will never know it until we respect ourselves, and relate our present, our past and our future."
C. L. R. James 1964

"Black people had moved from being packed 'like books upon a shelf' aboard the slave ship, to being authors, an extraordinary transformation and achievement, but even so, in terms of personal cost, a time of misery and confusion."
Paul Edwards & David Dabydeen *Black Writers in Britain 1760-1890* 1991

Black publishing in Britain goes back a long way. In the eighteenth century several books by black authors were published, for instance Gronniosaw's autobiography (c. 1770), Phillis Wheatley's poems (1773), Ignatius Sancho's letters (1782) and Cugoano's attack on slavery (1787). The most successful was the autobiography of Olaudah Equiano, which first appeared in 1789 and by 1794 was into its ninth edition. There were also editions published in America, Holland, Germany and Russia.

The work was entitled *The Interesting Narrative of the Life of Olaudah Equiano, or Gustavus Vassa, the African, Written by himself.* It was "printed for and sold by the author" and distributed by booksellers throughout the country. In the typical manner of publishing books in the eighteenth century, Equiano had gathered a list of subscribers who had paid him part of the cost of the book in order to finance the publication.

Olaudah Equiano, former slave, from the frontispiece to the original edition of his memoirs, 1789

Frontispiece of Phillis Wheatley's book of poems, London, 1773.

Subscribers to the first edition included the Prince of Wales and members of the aristocracy, as well as John Wesley, the founder of Methodism, who read the book on his death-bed. More significantly, Ottobah Cugoano, Hannah More, Thomas Clarkson and Granville Sharp were on the list. In 1783 it was Equiano who had drawn Sharp's attention to the massacre of 130 slaves aboard the 'Zong' off the West African coast, when they were "thrown alive into the sea".

In 1787 Sharp and Clarkson and a group of Quakers set up the Committee for Effecting the Abolition of the Slave Trade and started to distribute pamphlets against the slave trade throughout the country. This was at a time when 80,000 African slaves a year were being transported to the Americas, over half in British ships.

Equiano played a large part in the mass movement which developed over the next few years, when hundreds of petitions from around the country were presented to Parliament in support of abolition of the African slave trade, which was eventually achieved in 1807. His book is structured in the form of a petition, beginning with an address to members of Parliament. Most importantly, however, this was the first full account of slavery and the slave trade published by a former African slave.

In order to protect his copyright, Equiano registered his book with the Stationers' Company, and to publicise it he went on promotional tours throughout England, Ireland and Scotland, speaking out against the slave trade. He oversaw the production and distribution of all the editions produced during his lifetime and each edition contained a new list of subscribers.

Chapter 2

The History of Caribbean Publishing in Britain
Robert Wedderburn

"Truth is our polar star, to that we look for a safe passage to popularity."
Robert Wedderburn *The Forlorn Hope* 1817

"Wedderburn believed that an alliance of rebels across racial divisions would create a class-based revolt against international capitalism in all its manifestations. As well as the writing and dissemination of pamphlets and contributions to radical periodicals, Wedderburn preached sedition at political meetings to the radical working class."
Alan Rice *Radical Narratives of the Black Atlantic* 2003

After the slave trade was officially abolished in 1807, slavery itself was still rife in the West Indies and it was to take another 30 years to end it. One of the key campaigners against slavery was Robert Wedderburn, who was born in Jamaica in 1762 of a Scottish father and a Jamaican mother. He was the first Caribbean publisher in Britain. In 1817 he produced a couple of periodicals in London, one of which was called *The Forlorn Hope or A Call to the Supine, to rouse from Indolence and assert Public Rights.* The first issue explained that its aim was "to establish something in the shape of a free Press".

The second one was *The Axe Laid to the Root or A Fatal Blow to Oppressors*, which Wedderburn edited and published. It contained articles on religion and politics, reviews, letters and poems about slavery. Wedderburn knew about slavery – his

Robert Wedderburn

grandmother had been flogged almost to death and his mother had been raped by his slave-owning father. At the age of sixteen Wedderburn went to sea, ending up in England, where he became a tailor. He eventually joined a radical political group called the Spenceans, who believed in equality and restoring the land to the people.

Although only a handful of these publications were produced, Wedderburn managed to link the struggle against oppression in Britain to the fight against slavery in the West Indies. At the end of one article he wrote: "I am a West-Indian, a lover of liberty, and would dishonour human nature if I did not shew myself a friend to the liberty of others." He predicted that "the island of Jamaica will be in the hands of the blacks within twenty years. Prepare for flight, ye planters, for the fate of St. Domingo awaits you."

He became famous for the revolutionary rhetoric with which he entertained the crowds at Hopkins Street Chapel, which was a converted hayloft in Soho. The Home Secretary called him a "notorious firebrand" and his oratory was so powerful that he was put on the Government's secret list of 33 leading reformers. He was accused of sedition, but acquitted. Then he was re-arrested on a charge of blasphemy and in 1820 was sent to jail for two years.

When he came out, he continued his revolutionary activity and in 1824 he published his own autobiography entitled *The Horrors of Slavery*, in which he explained why he could not return to Jamaica: "I should have gone back to Jamaica, had I not been fearful of the planters; for such is their hatred of any one having black blood in his veins, and who dares to think and act as a free man, that they would most certainly have trumped up some charge against me, and hung me. With them I should have had no mercy."

He concludes his account by saying: "I thank my GOD, that through a long life of hardship and adversity, I have ever been free both in mind and body: and have always raised my voice in behalf of my enslaved countrymen!"

"I am a West-Indian, a lover of liberty, and would dishonour human nature if I did not shew myself a friend to the liberty of others."

Chapter 3

The History of Caribbean Publishing in Britain
Celestine Edwards

"The day is coming when Africans will speak for themselves. The day is breaking and the despised African, whose only crime is his colour, will yet give an account of himself. We think it no crime for Africans to look with suspicion upon the European, who has stolen a part of their country and deluged it with rum and powder, under the cover of civilisation."
Celestine Edwards *Lux* 18 February 1893

"The Mohammedans do try to make the people sober, which is a vast improvement upon our drunken colonies in Western Africa. It is true that we pretend to be going for the express purpose of putting down the slave trade, with a kind of righteous indignation and horror at the wickedness of the followers of Islam, when the truth is that we substitute a system which is worse than slavery." Celestine Edwards (1858-1894)

Celestine Edwards also started his life at sea. He was born in 1858 in Dominica, the youngest of ten children, and at the age of 12 stowed away on a French ship and became a seaman.

A story about him, written by his friend R. V. Allen, has Edwards say: "I was a knowing little nipper, and being the baby of the family, and undoubtedly spoilt by my sisters, as they couldn't do much with me at home they sent me to school in the neighbouring island of Antigua. But you know, when I was a youngster, school was one of the things I couldn't stand, and I made my mind up to do a bolt. There was but one way to go, and that was to sea, so to sea I went, and after that where I knocked

Portrait of Celestine Edwards from *Lux*, 29 July 1893

ANNIVERSARY NUMBER.

LUX

A WEEKLY

Christian Evidence Newspaper.

EDITED BY S. J. CELESTINE EDWARDS.

Publishing Offices: 18, PATERNOSTER ROW,

LONDON, E.C.

CONTENTS—

Vol. II. No. 52.   [Entered at Stationers' Hall.]   JULY 29, 1893.   [Transmission Abroad at Book Rates.]   TWOPENCE.

CHRISTIAN EVIDENCE SOCIETY.

REPORT, 1891-92.—Sermons and Lectures, 544. Open-air Lectures, 1891, 541; 1890, 548; 1889, 528. Open-air Stations, 20; attendance every Sunday about 6,000. Special Chr. Evid. Tracts and Handbills given away, 74,575. Students examined, 150; Prizes, 22; Certificates, 114; Receipts, £1,135; Expenditure, £1,158. Annual Income required to extend operations in the Provinces, £2,000. PLEASE CONTRIBUTE TO IT.

Offices: 13, BUCKINGHAM STREET, STRAND, W.C.

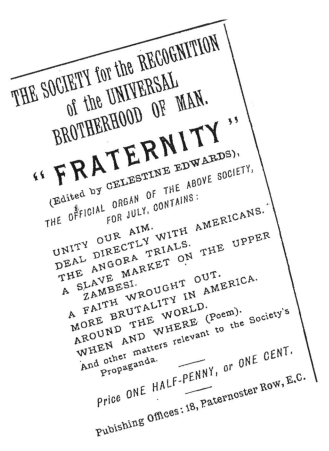

In the anniversary number, on 29 July 1893, 11,000 copies "went out of the office to different parts of the country". Edwards hoped to secure "a permanent circulation of over 10,000 a week". In 1893 he also published *Fraternity*, the monthly magazine of the Society for the Recognition of the Universal Brotherhood of Man, which reached a circulation of more than 7,000.

As well as editing these two papers, Celestine Edwards toured the country, speaking about racism, colonialism and lynching in America. In Newcastle, for example, he told an audience, on 3rd November 1894: "My ancestors proudly trod the sands of the African continent, but from their home and friends were dragged into the slave mart and sold to the planters of the West Indies. The very thought that my race should have been so grievously wronged is almost more than I can bear. Of the condition of my people today I but tarry to say that by diligence, thought and care they have given the lie to many a false prophet who, prior to their Emancipation, sought to convince the world that the black man was in all respects unfit for freedom. Their position today is one over which I proudly rejoice. To their future I look with confidence."

Edwards worked tirelessly for the cause. He also wanted to become a doctor and enrolled at the London Hospital, but his health was poor and in May 1894 he returned to his family in the West Indies to try and recover. He died there in his brother's arms on 25 July 1894. An obituary recalled: "He was proud of his colour and his people. He lived not for himself."

about, or where I did not go, I simply can't tell you. Once I nearly had my head smashed, and once I fell overboard, and the rows on shipboard and ashore I got into, weren't a few, I can tell you." Allen also describes Edwards as "a tall, well-built, powerful and handsome figure" and "an extraordinary personality".

In the 1870s he settled in Edinburgh and later lived in Sunderland, before moving to Hackney in London. Here he worked as a building labourer and made speeches in Victoria Park on such issues as slavery. As a Primitive Methodist, he also lectured on temperance and wrote religious pamphlets.

In 1892 Edwards became editor of *Lux*, a "weekly Christian Evidence Newspaper", and in an editorial, on 10 December 1892, he wrote about Britain's seizure of Uganda: "As long as such unrighteous deeds as cold-blooded murders are permitted under the British flag, as long as avarice and cupidity prompt the actions of a missionary nation, so long we shall protest against public money being spent in the interest of land-grabbers."

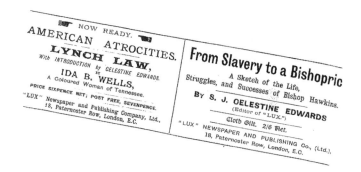

Chapter 4

The History of Caribbean Publishing in Britain
Henry Sylvester Williams

"Mr Williams was a man greatly esteemed by all with whom he came in contact and was held in great regard by the members of the profession to which he belonged and his death will be felt as a distinct loss to the community. He was a man who had a chequered and in some respects a brilliant career, but undoubtedly his name will longest be remembered and cherished by his own people for his great interest in their behalf, which culminated in the well-known Pan-African Congress." Randolph Richardson Mole *Port of Spain Mirror* 29 March 1911

"He was certain that black people were the equals of any set of humans; and he could point to a large number, including himself, who already had demonstrated the proposition. He sought justice and fair competition. He was, finally, a decent and generous man." J. R. Hooker 1975

Another West Indian soon took the place of Celestine Edwards in the field of publishing. His name was Henry Sylvester Williams, born on 19 February 1869 in the village of Arouca in Trinidad. His father had settled there from Barbados and worked as a wheelwright.

He qualified as a teacher at the early age of 17 and eventually came to London to study law. In 1897 he founded the African Association, whose aims included "to encourage a feeling of unity to facilitate friendly intercourse among Africans in general" and to circulate "accurate information on all subjects affecting their rights". Sylvester Williams was the

Henry Sylvester Williams

Association's secretary and its president was Rev Henry Mason Joseph from Antigua.

The following year Williams got married to a white woman, Agnes Powell, who was a member of the Temperance Society and came from Gillingham in Kent. In the same year he issued a circular calling for a world conference of black people, particularly those in "South Africa, West Africa and the West Indies". In 1899 he coined the term 'Pan-African' and in 1900 the Pan-African Conference committee, with Williams as general secretary and Joseph as chair, organised the first Pan-African Conference which took place at Westminster Town Hall in July.

Among the speakers were C. W. French from St Kitts demanding equal rights; John E. Quinlan from St Lucia arguing that capitalists were trying to enslave black people again, especially in South Africa; and William Myer, a Trinidadian medical student, who attacked pseudo-scientific racism for "trying to prove that negroes were worthless and depraved persons who had no right to live".

This first Pan-African Association did not last long, but it was to inspire the later Pan-African Congresses which took place in Paris in 1919, organised by W. E. B. DuBois, London in 1921 and 1923, and Manchester in 1945.

Also it did produce a journal called *The Pan-African,* launched by Williams in October 1901, which was designed to spread information "concerning the interests of the African and his descendants in the British Empire". The editorial of the first issue claimed that "no other but a Negro can represent the Negro" and that "the times demand the presence of that Negro to serve the deserving cause of a people the most despised and ill-used today".

The journal was short-lived, however, and only about half a dozen issues appeared. Williams became a barrister in 1902, probably the first of African descent to practise in Britain. In 1906 he joined the Fabian Society and won a seat on Marylebone borough council as a Progressive and Labour Party candidate. In 1908 he returned to Trinidad with his family and established a successful legal practice in Port-of-Spain. He died of a kidney ailment on 26 March 1911, leaving his wife and five children. She was not very well off and had to take in lodgers, one of whom was H. A. Nurse, George Padmore's father.

Another West Indian editor around this time was F. E. M. Hercules. Although born in Venezuela, Hercules grew up in Trinidad where his father was a civil servant. In 1918 he founded the Society of Peoples of African Origin which produced a monthly journal called the *African Telegraph*. Only a few issues appeared, but they did cover the race riots which took place in British ports in the spring of 1919. In particular the paper supported the unemployed black sailors who were being attacked in Glasgow, which was suffering a post-war economic depression.

"In 1899 he coined the term 'Pan-African' and in 1900 the Pan-African Conference committee, with Williams as general secretary and Joseph as chair, organised the first Pan-African Conference which took place at Westminster Town Hall in July."

Chapter 5

The History of Caribbean Publishing in Britain
Harold Moody and *The Keys*

"New eras demand new analyses, and London's Black press of the '30s and '40s does not and cannot provide stock solutions for today's problems, despite some striking similarities between past and present. But the determination of the Black writers and intellectuals of that generation to confront and expose problems and apply themselves to the hard task of analysis should remain an inspiration."
Roderick J. Macdonald *The wisers who are far away* 1992

> *"I am black,*
> *And so I must be*
> *More clever than white folk,*
> *More wise than white folk,*
> *More discreet than white folk,*
> *More courageous than white folk."*
> Una Marson *Black Burden* 1945

A more long-lasting journal was first produced in July 1933. This was *The Keys*, the official organ of the League of Coloured Peoples, whose president was Harold Moody from Jamaica. Moody was born in Kingston on 8 October 1882, the son of a pharmacist whose father was white. He came to London in 1904 to study medicine at King's College.

When he arrived, he discovered the colour bar operating in the country. He found it hard to get lodgings and was denied a hospital appointment because the matron "refused to have a coloured doctor working at the hospital". In February 1913 he started his own practice in Peckham and eventually

Harold Moody

The Official Organ of The League of Coloured Peoples

Vol. IV., No. 3.   Price 6d.   January-March, 1937.

made a success of it. In the same year he married a white woman, Olive Tranter, who was a nurse he had met while working on the wards of the Royal Eye Hospital and with whom he was to have six children.

Moody was also a Congregationalist lay preacher and a pacifist. His favourite text was from Paul's Epistle to the Galatians: "There is neither Jew nor Greek, there is neither bond nor free, there is neither male nor female: for ye are all one in Christ Jesus."

The League of Coloured Peoples (LCP) was founded on 13 March 1931. Members of the executive, largely from the Caribbean, included Dr Belfield Clark from Barbados, George Roberts from Trinidad, Samson Morris from Grenada and Robert Adams from Guyana. The Vice President was John Alexandra Barbour James, also from Guyana.

Among the organisation's aims were: "to promote and protect the Social, Educational, Economic and Political Interests of its members; to interest members in the Welfare of Coloured Peoples in all parts of the World; and to improve relations between the Races".

In July 1933 the League started publishing its quarterly magazine *The Keys*, whose one object was "to improve relations between the Races". The name came from the inspiration of the African Dr. Aggrey who asserted that the fullest musical harmony could be expressed only by the use of black and white keys on the piano.

It was initially edited by David Tucker from Bermuda, who wrote of striving for "the harmonious co-operation of the races". The first issue contained a poem entitled *Nigger*, by the Jamaican poet and broadcaster Una Marson, which began:

They called me "Nigger",
Those little white urchins,
They laughed and shouted
As I passed along the street,
They flung it at me:
"Nigger! Nigger! Nigger!"

What made me keep my fingers
From choking the words in their throats?

What made my face grow hot,
The blood boil in my veins
And tears spring to my eyes?
What made me go to my room
And sob my heart away
Because white urchins
Called me "Nigger"?

Una Marson in 1930

Some Members of the Cast "AT WHAT A PRICE"

Una Marson, second from left

Later editions were edited by different people, including Una Marson herself and Peter Blackman from Barbados. The famous Trinidadian historian C. L. R. James wrote an article on the West Indian cricket team which was touring England in 1933, and later in 1936 wrote one called 'Abyssinia and the Imperialists' after Mussolini's invasion of Ethiopia in October 1935. James's play *Toussaint L'Ouverture*, with Paul Robeson in the lead, was reviewed in the magazine, as was Robeson's address to the LCP on 'The Negro in the Modern World'. It was reported in 1935 that Robeson planned to open a permanent African theatre in London and his appearance at the Albert Hall on 19 January 1936, in front of an audience of 10,000 people, was also covered.

In January 1934 the League presented the Jamaican play *At What a Price*, by Una Marson and Horace Vaz, at the Scala Theatre. In November of the previous year it had been performed at the YMCA, with a cast of twenty. This was "the first time that a play written and performed by Coloured Colonials had been staged in London". Its first production, however, had been in Kingston,

Jamaica, in 1932. Una Marson, who lodged with Harold Moody in Peckham, when she first came to London, became famous for devising the BBC radio programme *Caribbean Voices* in 1943. Back in Jamaica, in 1949, she became the organising secretary for the Pioneer Press, Jamaica's first serious publishing house, which was the first to publish work by Louise Bennett in 1949.

There were inevitable conflicts amongst such a wide variety of contributors to the magazine. For example Moody and Marson, who was the daughter of a Baptist minister, had disagreements with Marxists like Blackman and James. Also Moody said he had to "appeal to the Africans and West Indians to cease bickering among themselves". For him too, coloured meant negro, so he opposed Asian membership of the League, despite the fact that white people could join. This resulted in discriminating, for instance, against half the population of Guyana who were of Indian origin.

Nevertheless, despite Harold Moody's paternalism, there were many areas of agreement, and campaigns were organised, for example, to

"THE KEYS"

The Official Organ of

The League of Coloured Peoples

Vol. 2. No. 3.   Price 6d.   January-March, 1935

Trip to Epsom in 1935

A group of youngsters off to Epsom in 1933

support the black seamen in Cardiff who were virtually all made unemployed in 1935. They had been classified as aliens and calls were made for their repatriation.

Similarly, when labour unrest broke out in the Trinidad oilfields in June 1937 and strikes took place in Jamaica the following year, *The Keys* supported the demonstrators. In an article in the journal, the St Lucian economist Arthur Lewis (later to become a Nobel Prize winner) attacked the report of the commission of inquiry into the Trinidad disturbances, and Moody had three letters published in *The Times* criticising police brutality in Jamaica.

Moody's philanthropic work extended to all the children born into Britain's black community. Each year he took coach-loads of the youngsters on a summer trip to Epsom and each year he organised a Christmas party for them.

With the outbreak of the Second World War, after having been published "without a break for nearly seven years", *The Keys* ceased publication and was replaced by a newsletter. The main concern of the first edition of October 1939 was to appeal for money for:

- A Christmas party for "any coloured children domiciled in London".
- Newcomers to this country – "Recently two students who arrived just before the war not only had to be met but also had to be evacuated to Devon".
- The Gold Coast earthquake, which "took place on June 20th, 1939 and mainly affected the principal town of the Gold Coast, namely Accra, causing great suffering, especially among the poor people, and damage estimated to approximately five million pounds".

Walter Tull

The *News Letter* also attacked the colour bar in the British armed forces, particularly the ban on commissions for black servicemen and women. When the ban was lifted for the period of the war, Moody wrote: "We are thankful for this, but we are not satisfied. We do not want it only for the duration of the war. We want it for all time. If the principal is accepted now, surely it must be acceptable all the time."

It was also pointed out that Walter Tull had been the "first coloured officer in the British Army" when he was commissioned in 1917. His father was a carpenter from Barbados who married an Englishwoman. Tull fought in Italy and France and was killed in the second battle of the Somme on 25 March 1918. He was awarded the British War and Victory medal and recommended for a Military Cross.

The *News Letter* continued up until 1951, although Harold Moody had died in 1947. Contributors included George Padmore and Learie Constantine.

"Tull fought in Italy and France and was killed in the second battle of the Somme on 25 March 1918. He was awarded the British War and Victory medal and recommended for a Military Cross."

Chapter 6

The History of Caribbean Publishing in Britain
Marcus Garvey and the *Black Man*

"Always remember that the press is a mighty power." Marcus Garvey *Black Man* July 1935

"The stone that the builder refused shall be the head cornerstone." Psalms 118:22

"Emancipate yourself from mental slavery, none but ourselves can free our minds." Marcus Garvey, October 1937

Marcus Garvey was born in St. Ann's Bay, Jamaica, on 17 August 1887. His father was a mason and a deacon in the Methodist Church; his mother a domestic worker and farmer. He had to leave school at the age of fourteen to help support his family.

He went to Kingston to become a printer, which was to help him in his numerous publications. In 1908 he took part in a strike by printers and was fired from his job. The following year his newspaper *The Watchman* began publication, but only lasted for three issues

Most of Garvey's life was spent in America where he built up the largest African American mass movement in American history – the Universal Negro Improvement Association, whose aim was "the general uplift of the Negro peoples of the world". He lectured in liberty halls across the United States to audiences of tens of thousands of people, greeted by tumultuous applause.

In 1918 he founded a weekly newspaper called *Negro World* in which many of his speeches and essays appeared. It enjoyed a circulation of nearly a quarter of a million readers.

Marcus Garvey

Hansib Publications, 1997

His 'Back to Africa' slogan was aimed at restoring respect for African culture among black Americans and, long before the Civil Rights Movement, he said: "I shall teach the black man to see beauty in himself."

He eventually returned to Kingston, where he founded a magazine called the *Black Man* in December 1933. In 1935 he travelled to London where he continued its publication. In every issue he carried on his campaign on behalf of the Ethiopian resistance to Italian occupation, including his own poems, such as *Il Duce – The Brute* and *The Smell of Mussolini*. The magazine also contained articles by the Guyanese short-story writer Eric Walrond who had settled in England in 1932. The *Black Man* circulated widely, in the USA, the West Indies, Central America and Africa.

One innovation Garvey introduced was a series of dramatic dialogues, often between black and white characters, such as the one between a white lady heckler and a Negro speaker at Hyde Park Corner, where Garvey himself used to speak (and was heckled by the left-wing Trinidadian C. L. R. James!).

Another was a conversation between a father and son about African civilisation:

Son: "Must I take it that the Negro will ultimately emancipate himself through the development of his own mind?"

Father: "Yes, all emancipation is from within. That is to say, real emancipation. As a man thinketh so is he. That means that the man must think for himself and make himself."

Son: "I have been very much worried, father, over Africa's past and present, in that I know so very little of it; yet I am considered by blood an African."

Father: "Africa's history, my boy, is really not written, and so you may know very little of the past by the reading of present-day books."

Although the *Black Man* appeared irregularly, Marcus Garvey continued its publication, from Beauchamp Street in Fulham, up until just before his death on 10 June, 1940, aged 52. He was buried in Kensal Green Cemetery, London. On 15 November, 1964, however, the government of Jamaica proclaimed him Jamaica's first national hero and had his remains brought from England and placed in a shrine in National Heroes Park.

Although he died in relative obscurity, he later had a great influence on the Black Power and Civil Rights movements and on Rastafarianism. His memory is kept alive through reggae artists such as Burning Spear, Mighty Diamonds and Bob Marley.

Bob Marley

The History of Caribbean Publishing in Britain
Ras T. Makonnen

"We base ourselves upon the great masses of the people. The individual achievements of a few black men do not and cannot solve the problem of the blacks. One of our most important tasks is to make clear to the black intellectuals and other members of the middle class, that in the present state of world affairs there is no way out for them by seeking crumbs from the tables of their imperialist masters. They must identify themselves with the struggle of the masses."
C. L. R. James *International African Opinion* July 1938

Like Harold Moody, Ras T. Makonnen straddled the Second World War with his publishing activity. He was born George Thomas Nathaniel Griffith in the village of Buxton, Guyana, around 1900. (Buxton was named after the British MP Thomas Buxton who took over the anti-slavery campaign from Wilberforce in 1823.) After spending some time in America, he settled in London in 1937 and then moved to Manchester, where he established a chain of restaurants and a night-club.

Makonnen's business skills were based on his upbringing in Guyana: "I think a lot of the success of these ventures could be attributed to the fact that I was no stranger to business. My early orientation in Guyana, the observation I had made of my father in the diamond industry meant that I was prepared to venture where someone with no background would hesitate."

His aim, however, was not merely financial, but political: "But I did not regard these restaurants as

Ras T. Makonnen

"Buxton was named after the British MP Thomas Buxton who took over the anti-slavery campaign from Wilberforce in 1823."

Published by The International African Service Bureau in 1945

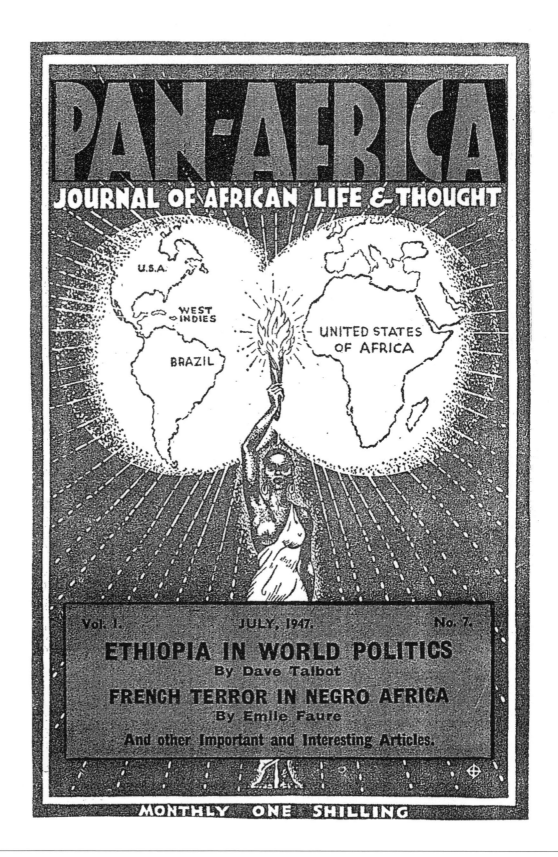

George Padmore

Jomo Kenyatta

mine, nor the takings for that matter. This was what the pan-African thing was all about. I suppose I felt that they made it possible to carry on a whole range of defence operations for blacks at home and abroad."

His profits enabled him to set up the Pan-African Publishing Company, whose directors included C. L. R. James and George Padmore, and to open a bookshop called the Economist in Oxford Road, Manchester. In 1936 he helped set up the International African Service Bureau, with Padmore as chair and himself as secretary. They produced a short-lived duplicated paper called *Africa and the World*. Makonnen also financed a monthly journal *International African Opinion*, edited by C. L. R. James.

Makonnen describes how he sold this publication: "With the paper printed I would then look up the halls where leftist meetings or peace meetings were on that night, and sell this thing illegally at the door on the way out. I would make pounds and pounds this way, because many an old English lady would give me ten shillings just to get rid of me. The other place I sold a large number was after speaking in Hyde Park. So sometimes I would clear more than £20 worth in a single meeting. After paying the printers, there would be still large savings, and I gradually built up capital without the other fellows noticing."

The journal only lasted a year, partly because of its radical stance. According to George Padmore: "The journal excited alarm in official quarters and was banned by East African colonial governments as 'seditious'." It was "finally forced to close down so as not to jeopardize the liberties of subscribers who were made liable to imprisonment if found reading the magazine".

After the War Makonnen helped organise and finance the Fifth Pan-African Congress in

Manchester in October 1945, and in January 1947 founded the monthly periodical *Pan-Africa*. He was the Publishing and Managing Editor, and associate editors included Jomo Kenyatta, Kwame Nkrumah and H. W. Springer from Barbados.

An editorial in the July issue states: "Our readers, united in a common African consciousness, are widely scattered: their lives and problems are different and they know little of one another. Can we not introduce them? A few short, vivid descriptive sketches which would show a West Indian student how a Gold Coast farmer lives, or make a Buganda feel the meaning of industrial troubles in Johannesburg, would be as valuable as political discussions in creating a common understanding."

A double issue in January/February 1948 concentrated on African Americans, with contributions from W. E. B. Du Bois and Langston Hughes. But in spring of that year the publication ceased.

Kwame Nkrumah

"Our readers, united in a common African consciousness, are widely scattered: their lives and problems are different and they know little of one another. Can we not introduce them?"

Chapter 8
The History of Caribbean Publishing in Britain
Caribbean News

Growing Militancy in Guiana

from CHEDDI JAGAN

Two years ago in October the elected Government of the Peoples' Progressive Party of British Guiana was forcibly dissolved and the Constitution, granted only six months earlier, was smashed by Britain's Imperialist Government.

On the anniversary of this foul deed, Cheddi Jagan, leader of the P.P.P. contributes this article.

THE first significant event on the labour front since the suspension of the British Guiana Constitution and the expulsion of the Government formed by the Peoples' Progressive Party in October, 1953, is the recent strike of the Sawmill Workers. More than 1200 workers downed tools, and closed all the major sawmills in the city of Georgetown, the capital of British Guiana.

Negotiations with the Employers' organisation, the Forest Products Associations, reached a deadlock. Sawmill and Forest Workers' Union, on behalf workers, had put forward a 5-point demand, included a daily wage of $3.52 (14s. 8d.)

The Sawmill Workers' demand for $3.52 per day is in line with the wage claim recently made by the Federation of Unions of Government Employees. Despite the strong arguments put up based on the above facts, the Government, about two months ago, agreed to pay a minimum of only $2.52 per day, however, making it retro-active to January 1954.

Georgetown.—The police have refused Dr. Jagan, deposed premier of this country, and leader of the Peoples' Progressive Party, permission to travel to London to attend a conference of the Movement for Colonial Freedom. This organisation is supported by several Members of Parliament, local Labour Parties, co-op guilds, and trade unions.

Police have also refused to vary restrictions on Dr. Jagan, which limit his movements, even for the care of his patients, to the boundaries of the city of Georgetown.

CARIBBEAN NEWS 6d.

OCTOBER ★ ★ **1955**

What was the real reason for sacking Jamaican preacher?

NEWS last month that Dr. J. L. Wilson, Bishop of Birmingham, would not confirm the appointment of Dr. Marcus James to a local diocese, came as a low blow to all West Indians.

"Caribbean News" reported Dr. Marcus James' projected appointment in our May 1955 issue.

The brilliant Jamaican Doctor of Divinity has already made his mark on the international level, and his appointment to a Birmingham locality was some mark of respect shown at least by the church. Here was a man who could from his office and wide experience help to smooth the many rough edges that

WOW!! — Some Friendship!

"During its relatively short life, Caribbean News fulfilled an important role for West Indian activists both in Britain and in the Caribbean. It was banned as subversive material in most West Indian islands, much to the delight of the editorial team in London, who considered a ban by such anti-progressive forces to be a compliment to their political views. Despite the ban, ways and means were found of getting the paper through to our comrades at home." Trevor Carter *Shattering Illusions* 1986

In November 1952 the first issue of *Caribbean News* appeared, published by the London Branch of the Caribbean Labour Congress, with its stated aim: "Caribbean News has been created as a link in a strong chain to securely bind the oppressors of the West Indian people. It shall illuminate the dark corners by printing the truth." It started off monthly and then came out bi-monthly. The journal ran for 30 editions, with the last one, in June 1956, containing an interview with Claudia Jones.

Richard Hart

In October 1955, under the headline 'Black and White Together', the paper reported on the month-long strike at the Ann Shelley clothing factory in Stepney, east London: "They are refusing to work subject to the abuse, insults and vile language from a floor manager." The firm refused to do anything about it or to negotiate with the trade union: "This strike is demonstrating in action the unity of the workers, black and white, of English, West Indian, and Pakistani men and women." 125 workers were involved, of whom twenty were black: "Mr H. Regal, factory convenor, told me, 'It's really remarkable to see coloured women earning £5 or £6 a week and having to pay around £2 5s a week for a single furnished room, paying bus fares and coming across London regularly to stand in the picket line.'"

The Caribbean Labour Congress (CLC) was founded in 1945 as a coalition of political groupings mainly from the English-speaking West Indian islands. Its general secretary was the radical Jamaican Richard Hart and it was supported by communists such as Billy Strachan, also from Jamaica, and Trevor Carter from Trinidad. The main objectives of the CLC were to fight for national liberation and to develop the idea of a Federation of the West Indies. It was supported by most active West Indian trade unionists, particularly in London.

Caribbean News encouraged West Indian workers to join a trade union and supported industrial action, such as the successful dockers' strike in 1954: "For 28 days the port workers of Britain have been on strike, in the biggest stoppage in British labour history since the General Strike in 1926. This militant action by the dockers in defence of their elementary rights has ended in victory for them. Their strike was no picnic as some tend to think, but involved severe sacrifice by the men, their wives and children. The Caribbean Labour Congress (London Branch) was privileged to make a contribution of £2 to the strike fund, and in this small way to show the solidarity of West Indian workers with their British comrades."

"They are refusing to work subject to the abuse, insults and vile language from a floor manager." The firm refused to do anything about it or to negotiate with the trade union: "This strike is demonstrating in action the unity of the workers, black and white, of English, West Indian, and Pakistani men and women." 125 workers were involved, of whom twenty were black ..."

Internationally *Caribbean News* campaigned for African liberation, particularly in Kenya; and in the West Indies it supported the People's Progressive Party in what was then British Guiana. In October, 1955, for example, Cheddi Jagan reported on a sawmill workers strike in the capital Georgetown, when "more than 1200 workers downed tools". This edition also recorded: "The police have refused Dr. Jagan, deposed premier of this country, and leader of the People's Progressive Party, permission to travel to London to attend a conference of the Movement for Colonial Freedom."

In *Shattering Illusions*, Trevor Carter sums up the impact of the paper in Britain: "Looking back at the editions of *Caribbean News*, a picture emerges of Britain which is not only the untold story of the black trade unionists of the time, but is also an insight into that part of the whole trade union and labour movement which had contact with us. It shows that there were pockets within the movement which, thanks to the combination of enlightened leadership and the influence of a black perspective, had broadened its view of its own role and interests away from the narrow 'bread-and-butter' outlook which has tended to dominate over most of the past thirty years."

"The police have refused Dr. Jagan, deposed premier of this country, and leader of the People's Progressive Party, permission to travel to London to attend a conference of the Movement for Colonial Freedom."

Chapter 9

The History of Caribbean Publishing in Britain
Claudia Jones and the
West Indian Gazette

"The West Indian Gazette was the 'parent' of all papers published since 1958." Buzz Johnson *I Think of My Mother* 1985

"The Gazette was therefore not only timely, but also a vital medium of communication within the black community and, as the black population increased, the Gazette played an even more important role through its advertisements, which included announcements of various meetings, steamship travel to and from the Caribbean, information about West Indian shops, clubs, restaurants and services in London; and, significantly, organised the first 'Caribbean Carnival' in Notting Hill in January 1959." Ron Ramdin *Reimaging Britain* 1999

"The West Indian Gazette, like a child from the insalubrious part of town, was born into a struggle and its life was destined to be short, tortuous, and somewhat bruising." Donald Hinds *Journey to an Illusion* 1966

The political perspective of *Caribbean News* was carried forward by Claudia Jones. She published the first edition of the *West Indian Gazette* "as a one leaf flyer in March 1958". (It later changed its name to the *West Indian Gazette & Afro-Asian-Caribbean News.*)

Claudia was born on 21 February 1915 in Port of Spain, Trinidad, but in 1922 her parents emigrated to New York and two years later she and her three sisters joined them. The family was very poor and their apartment so damp that in 1932 Claudia contracted tuberculosis.

Claudia Jones

Journey

to an

Illusion

The West Indian in Britain

.Donald Hinds

HEINEMANN : LONDON

"There are fewer than half a dozen West Indians in the United Kingdom who are making a living entirely by practising journalism. One or two have got into the foreign service of liberal newspapers. Other journals with interest in the Caribbean have from time to time employed West Indian journalists for short periods. In the main, West Indian contributions to British Journals are on either cricket or the coloured community. So most journalists from the Caribbean are either practising novelists or copious writers of short stories.

"The professional writer from the Caribbean has got to be read in Britain if he is to survive. There is no loyal readership in the West Indies. Subsequently many of the West Indian novelists live and write in such places as New York, London and Paris."

Journey to an Illusion: The West Indian in Britain by Donald Hinds 1966

Claudia with Cheddi Jagan

Kelso Cochrane

After leaving school, she began to write for a Harlem journal and in 1936 joined the Communist Party, editing a number of their papers. In January 1948 she was arrested for the first time and threatened with deportation to Trinidad. She was accused of teaching and advocating the overthrow of the US Government by force.

Further trials and imprisonment took their toll on Claudia and she suffered heart failure. Her final period in prison ended in 1955 and she was then deported to Britain where she continued to suffer ill-health.

It was the West Indian Workers and Students Association which set up an editorial committee to publish a paper and Claudia was chosen as editor. The summer of 1958 saw a series of racial attacks in Britain, particularly in Nottingham and Notting Hill, London. George Lamming commented in the *Gazette*: "Here all the niceties of cricket came to an end. I don't think that we have heard the last word from Notting Hill." The paper was threatened by the Ku Klux Klan of Britain and in August they trashed its office in Brixton, south London.

The office, however, became an international cultural and political focus in London, attracting such figures as Paul Robeson, Norman Manley and Cheddi Jagan. Writers such as George Lamming, Jan Carew, Andrew Salkey and Sam Selvon visited the office and gave support to the paper.

The *Gazette* could not afford to pay its staff, so they all had other jobs too. Two of the early reporters were Donald Hinds, from Jamaica, and Ken Kelly, from Trinidad. Hinds worked as a bus conductor and Kelly as a typist for a news agency.

Circulation peaked at 30,000 during the winter of 1958, but then settled down to around 10,000. The paper was always in financial difficulties, not attracting enough advertising revenue, and it continually had to change printers. Nevertheless it continued to campaign politically and became the voice of black people in Britain. On 17 May 1959 Kelso Cochrane, an Antiguan carpenter, was murdered by six white people in Notting Hill. The *Gazette* helped organise the protests, though in the end no one was ever arrested.

Claudia became the most well-known campaigner on black issues, as Sheila Patterson

West Indian Gazette

and Afro - Asian Caribbean News

DEC-JAN 1965   6d.

VOL.. 7 No. I

Founded by the late Claudia Jones, 1958

CLAUDIA JONES' LAST EDITORIAL

Dr Luther King's warning

Dr. Martin Luther King, widely regarded as a "moderate" in his native America, where he is a leader in the mounting Negro peoples struggle for equality and freedom, had some excellent, and, for some, very radical things to say when passing through London on his way to Oslo to receive his Nobel Peace Prize.

What he said on racial discrimination caught the nations headlines, and intrigued the overwhelming majority of Commonwealth citizens from Asia, Africa and the Caribbean. As well it might, midst of a debate on renewal challenge to

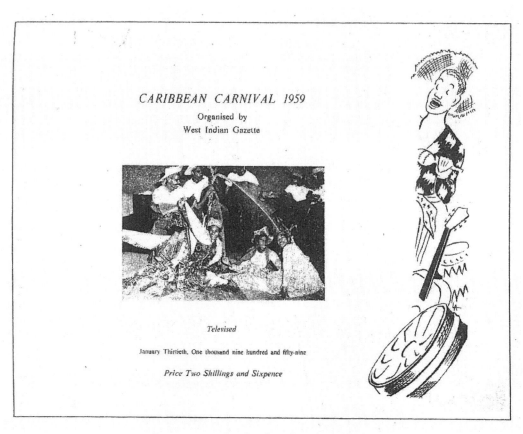

Programme for the first Carnival 1959

acknowledges in *Dark Strangers*, her book about West Indian migrants in Brixton, published in 1963: "With the possible exception of the journalist who edits the locally published monthly, *The West Indian Gazette*, no individual or group had even by the end of 1960 achieved the position of being known to the majority of settled migrants, still less of being able to exert any influence on their actions."

In her editorial of November 1959, Claudia wrote: "In some respects it is amazing how short people's memories are. A charitable view might ascribe this to the fact that the human mind tends to reject unpleasant facts. But much as we would like to forget unpleasant facts, we cannot fail to observe that the aftermath of Notting Hill is continuing in insidious ways. In the past several weeks in Britain West Indians and other peoples of colour have been victims of racial prejudice and colour bar practices. Take the recent case of Joseph Dill Simon of Notting Hill, formerly of Portsmouth, Dominica, who was walking quietly with a friend to catch a breath of fresh air, on an evening in October, when he was summarily shot in the wrist, at the corner of Talbot Road. He said: 'I know the police do not believe me, but a white man fired at me, because I am coloured.'"

The paper also organised cultural events, concerts, benefits and talent contests. Most famously, in November 1958, it sponsored a Caribbean Carnival Committee which, on Friday 30 January 1959, mounted the first Caribbean Carnival, at St. Pancras Town Hall in London. It went on to become the Notting Hill Carnival, the largest street festival in Europe, regularly attracting two million participants every August Bank Holiday.

In the 1959 carnival brochure, Claudia Jones wrote: "It is as if the vividness of our national life was itself the spark urging translation to new surroundings, to convey, to transplant our folk origins to British soil. There is comfort in this effort not only for the Carnival Committee and the *West*

Indian Gazette and for the fine artists participating in our Carnival who have lent of their talents here, but for all West Indians, who strain to feel and hear and reflect their idiom even as they strain to feel the warmth of their sun-drenched islands and its immemorable beauty of landscape and terrain."

As well as campaigning on British issues, such as the Commonwealth Immigration Act of 1962, the *Gazette* also addressed international matters, such as apartheid in South Africa, civil rights in America and the West Indies Federation.

In 1964 Martin Luther King, on his way to Oslo to collect his Nobel Peace Prize, called to see Claudia. Her comments on that meeting were to form her last editorial for the paper. She wrote: "The lessons of the American Negro struggle are that whatever advances towards equal rights and integration have been made, they have been accomplished in unity and struggle."

By this time she was living in a two-room flat on the ground floor at 58 Lisburne Road, Gospel Oak, north London. But on Christmas Eve 1964 she died in her sleep of a massive heart attack, aged 48. Her body was only discovered two days later when an upstairs neighbour, not getting any response at the door, broke a window and climbed in.

Claudia's cremation took place at Golders Green Crematorium on 9 January 1965 and among the many speeches there was a recorded message from Paul Robeson, which included the words: "The death of Claudia Jones is a great loss to us on this side of the Atlantic, and to you on your side. Many friends and comrades here grieve for her and are saddened by her loss. We send you our sad and sympathetic greetings, and it helps us to know that her work will continue through the Committee of Afro-Asian-Caribbean Organisations which she had built." The funeral concluded with Nadia Cattouse singing 'We Shall Overcome'. Her ashes were buried in Highgate Cemetery and nearly 20 years later a memorial stone was set up next to that of Karl Marx.

Only a few more issues of the Gazette came out. In February 1965 there was a memorial edition to Claudia which contained a tribute from Raymond Kunene of the African National Congress: "The death of Claudia Jones has deprived the liberation movement all over the world of one of the most dynamic and most militant fighters. It is difficult to think of anyone who in recent years has remained so incorruptible in spite of all the insidious influences of artificial independence. Claudia belonged to the forefront of the struggle against imperialism, colonialism and fascism."

The last issue was April-May which also had a double-page memorial to Claudia.

Beryl Gilroy, the Guyanese teacher and writer, came to Britain around the same time as Claudia. She calls her one of the "great women of fifties London who tore down the barricades of inhumanity and who tried to bring cohesion to the lives of the working class West Indians through her newspaper".

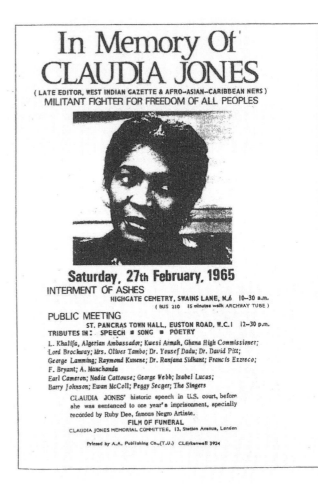

"By this time she was living in a two-room flat on the ground floor at 58 Lisburne Road, Gospel Oak, north London. But on Christmas Eve 1964 she died in her sleep of a massive heart attack, aged 48."

British 2008 Postage Stamp

Chapter 10

The History of Caribbean Publishing in Britain
Edward Scobie:
Tropic and *Flamingo*

"It is my belief that the thousands of coloured people here have a right to express their views; have a right to read the news from an unbiased viewpoint; have a right to a knowledge of the facts as they really are."
Edward Scobie *Flamingo* October 1961

"It was only long years after that I understood the limitation on spirit, vision and self-respect which was imposed on us by the fact that our masters, our curriculum, our code of morals, everything began from the basis that Britain was the source of all light and leading, and our business was to admire, wonder, imitate, learn; our criterion of success was to have succeeded in approaching that distant ideal – to attain it was, of course, impossible."
C. L. R. James *Beyond a Boundary* 1963

A different kind of magazine publishing was undertaken during this period of the early 1960s by Edward Scobie, who was born in Dominica in 1918. In 1960 he teamed up with Jamaican businessman Charles I. Ross and with Patrick Williams to produce the monthly *Tropic*. It announced itself as "the voice of 250,000 coloured people in Britain" and claimed: "We stand for coloured people everywhere in their struggle for Independence. In their fight to live with dignity and freedom."

In the June 1960 issue there was an article entitled 'Who Killed Kelso?' And Scobie recounts an incident which illustrates the dangers of the time: "In 1960, a shot was fired through the windows of the

Edward Scobie, *Flamingo* October 1961

Cy Grant on television as Othello, *Tropic* March 1960

Sculpture by Ronald Moody, *Tropic* August 1960

editorial offices of *Tropic* magazine, presumably intended for the editor who had only just left the room. An editorial comment in the magazine noted that "although the incident was reported to the police, no result of the investigation was ever reported".

As well as dealing with political events in Africa and the West Indies, there were all the ingredients of a modern magazine: sport, music, recipes, photography, beauty, baby care, hairdressing, fashion and design. There were articles on the Trinidadian pianist Winifred Atwell, Cy Grant from Guyana, rock singer Ricky Wayne from St. Lucia, Shirley Bassey and Cleo Laine.

Scobie was particularly interested in the history of black people in Britain and later produced a book dealing with the subject, called *Black Britannia*. In *Tropic* he used his research to write about famous figures such as the musician George Bridgtower, the celebrated 19th-century actor Ira Aldridge and the composer Samuel Coleridge-Taylor. He also pointed out that the "arrival of coloured students to Britain began as long ago as 1554".

There were short stories in the magazine, by writers such as Samuel Selvon and Jan Carew, and articles by George Lamming and Donald Hinds. A review was published of a television production of Errol John's Trinidadian play *Moon on a Rainbow Shawl*, with its "all-Negro" cast, "the first play written by a West Indian to be televised in Britain".

Sculpture featured often: a Nigerian sculptor making chess sets, the maroon sculptor Namba Roy and, also from Jamaica, Ronald Moody (Harold Moody's brother). Reference was made to a proposal to form a New Negro Theatre Company by Jamaican Clifton Jones, using the Theatre Royal, Stratford, in east London.

Despite its vibrant cultural and political content, however, *Tropic* only lasted till the end of the year. It was replaced in September 1961 by *Flamingo*, also edited by Edward Scobie. Among its special correspondents were Jan Carew and Marcia Gregg from Guyana. The magazine noted the 350,000 West Indians then living in Britain and stated: "Up till now these Negro citizens of Britain have been denied a Voice." The second issue in October

Paul Robeson reading the magazine, *Tropic* July 1960

Ancient print of Aesop, *Flamingo* April 1963

Flamingo October 1961

Flamingo June 1962

MOTHERS! HERE'S HOW TO BUILD HEALTH INTO YOUR BABIES' FUTURE

We all know perfect health is one of nature's most precious gifts to our children. But did you know that you can *build* health for your babies' future? Seven Seas Cod Liver Oil every day is the best way to do it. Seven Seas helps prevent all chest ailments; gives vim, vitamins and vigour. Replaces energy expended during play. Build health and energy into your children's future the rich, *natural* way — with golden Seven Seas Cod Liver Oil.

Seven Seas
RICH GOLDEN COD LIVER OIL

Flamingo June 1963

claimed that 20,000 copies had been sold in Britain and 15,000 in America.

Scobie wrote articles on such figures as Ignatius Sancho and Olaudah Equiano. He explained the African origins of Aesop and compared black street cleaners of today with those in the eighteenth century. He also discussed the significance of the case of the runaway slave James Somerset who was recaptured by his master who wanted to take him back to Jamaica. The case came to court and after lengthy proceedings Lord Chief Justice Mansfield finally decreed: "No master was ever allowed here to take a slave by force to be sold abroad because he deserted from his service... and therefore the man must be discharged."

Politics was dealt with, featuring, for example, Martin Luther King, Kwame Nkrumah, Kenneth Kaunda and the fascist leader Oswald Mosley, who was still active at that time. The November 1961 issue reported the Jamaican vote (251,935 to 216,400) to leave the West Indies Federation. And a piece entitled 'British Guiana's Dilemma' appeared in June 1962, which concluded: "It is unfortunate that the three leaders of the country belong to different ethnic groups. Dr. Jagan is Indian, Mr. Burnham is Negro and Mr. D'Aguiar is Portuguese."

There was also an emphasis on Africa, with articles on such countries as Tunisia, Ghana, Tanganyika, Sierra Leone and Angola. Sport was covered too, including horse-racing, wrestling, athletics, football and cricket, with an article by the famous Trinidadian all-rounder Learie Constantine who had recently been made high commissioner for Trinidad and Tobago.

There was a strong cultural element in the magazine, including reviews and short stories by Jan Carew (Guyana), Sam Selvon (Trinidad) and George Lamming (Barbados). There were pieces on

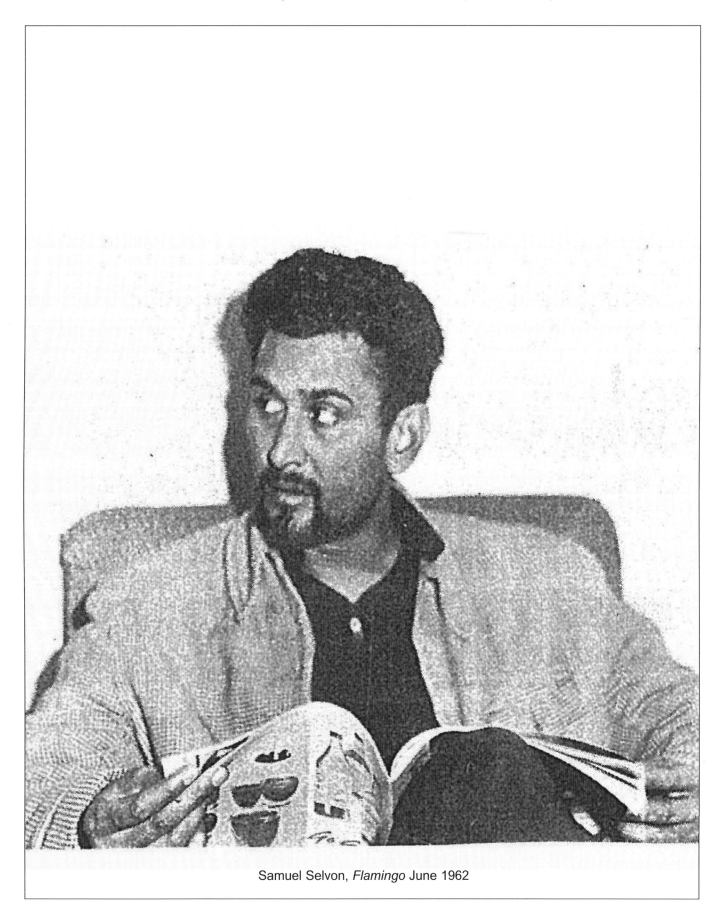

Samuel Selvon, *Flamingo* June 1962

George Lamming, *Flamingo* June 1963

(Cricketer)   (High Commissioner)

Flamingo June 1963

the Bermudan actor Earl Cameron, the Trinidadian jazz singer Billie Lane, Jamaican tenor Lloyd Ansel, Trinidadian film director Edric Connor and Jamaican poet Louise Bennett.

Flamingo was partly financed by advertisements, for example for life insurance, family planning, hairdressers and car dealers. Medicines featured prominently, such as Rose Hip Syrup and Seven Seas Cod Liver Oil, as did alcohol like Red Stripe and Appleton Rum.

Just before *Flamingo* closed in June 1963, another publication made a brief appearance for a few issues. This was *Daylight International*, subtitled 'The Negro News Magazine', aiming at providing news from Africa and the Caribbean. It was edited by Aubrey Baynes from St. Vincent, who claimed it was "not the mouthpiece of any political movement".

The first edition had a cover reproduction of a black Jesus on the cross, painted by the South African artist Ronald Harrison. The editorial records the mood of revolt in African, America and the Caribbean: "Our world is rife with revolution. My own, dear sweet revolution. It is the Negro Revolt. And it is an urgent thing! It is vital, most necessary, and now it begs of each of us to state; 'I want my freedom! I want equality! I want them now!'"

The final issue in August contained book reviews of *Beyond a Boundary* by C. L. R. James, *A Kind of Homecoming* by E. R. Braithwaite and two books by the Nigerian author Wole Soyinka. There had also earlier been mention of the West Indian actor Errol John playing Othello at the Old Vic.

In February1965, just before leaving for Canada, Jan Carew produced five issues of the *Magnet*, a radical black fortnightly, aiming to be the "Voice of the Afro-Asian Caribbean Peoples". Earlier in 1952 Carew had been a columnist on the *Kensington Post* and between 1953 and 1959 was a member of the Laurence Olivier company, acting in London, Liverpool and New York. The paper claimed to sell 25,000 copies and have a readership of over a quarter of a million. It contained book reviews by the Guyanese novelist Wilson Harris and reported the curfew imposed on C. L. R. James when he returned to Trinidad to report on the test cricket. George Lamming said it was "by far the most promising and exciting newspaper of its kind I have seen in England for twenty years". The last issue appeared in April. It was followed in May by *Caribbean Times* which claimed to be "the biggest West Indian weekly", but after three issues it folded.

Chapter 11

The History of Caribbean Publishing in Britain
New Beacon

"Growing up in a colonial society made John La Rose acutely aware that colonial policy was based on a deliberate withholding of information from the population. There was a discontinuity of information from generation to generation. Publishing therefore, was a vehicle to give an independent validation to one's own culture, history, politics – a sense of self – and to make a break with the discontinuity." New Beacon Books Publishing Catalogue 2007

"Small publishing house perhaps but no small achievement for an expatriate (Trinidadian-born) intellectual and his English wife to establish a medium for Caribbean and other writers of cross-cultural merit in Africa or the Americas when the metropolitan scene is extremely competitive and there is a dearth of publishing ventures of repute in the West Indies." Wilson Harris *Foundations of a Movement* 1991

The end of the 1960s saw an important development in Caribbean publishing in Britain with the foundation of two publishing houses: New Beacon Books and Bogle-L'Ouverture Press.

New Beacon was founded in August 1966, at the same time as the formation of the Caribbean Artists Movement, by John La Rose with the active support and assistance of Sarah White. (It was named after the influential magazine The Beacon, produced in Trinidad in 1931, with contributors such as C. L. R. James.) Its first publication was a book of La Rose's poems. The following year New Beacon went into book-selling and gradually built up its shop in north

John La Rose

New Beacon Bookshop, Stroud Green Road, Finsbury Park, North London

London to make books on the black experience widely available. In 1971 they reissued C. L. R. James's *Minty Alley* and in 1977 published Martin Carter's *Poems of Succession.*

John La Rose had come to Britain in 1961, from Trinidad, where he was an anti-colonial activist in the Workers Freedom Movement and later the West Indian Independence Party, and also involved in the trade union movement. In London he was the director of the first International Book Fair of Radical, Black and Third World Books.

New Beacon developed first as a specialist bookseller, producing the first ever catalogues of Caribbean materials combining works in English, French and Spanish. Later catalogues combined materials from the Caribbean, black Britain, Africa and African America.

John La Rose died in 2006, but his partner Sarah White and Janice Durham, who was born in Grenada, continue to run the book-shop and publish their monthly list of books, which is an invaluable resource. Also historical materials, built up over the years, are kept in the George Padmore Institute, above the shop in Stroud Green Road.

"New Beacon developed first as a specialist bookseller, producing the first ever catalogues of Caribbean materials combining works in English, French and Spanish."

Chapter 12

The History of Caribbean Publishing in Britain
Bogle-L'Ouverture

"We think it's fairly well known that the founding of Bogle-L'Ouverture Publications was based on a corporate decision to make a total break with the usual tradition of publishing: that of Black people passively providing the human material to be written up and published by other people."
Jessica Huntley 1975

In 1969, Eric and Jessica Huntley founded Bogle-L'Ouverture Publications, after arriving in Britain from Guyana in the late 1950s, and in 1974 opened their bookshop in Ealing, west London. Their press was named after Paul Bogle, who led the Morant Bay Rebellion in Jamaica, and Toussaint L'Ouverture, leader of the successful slave rebellion in San Domingo (Haiti). The bookshop was later named

Eric and Jessica Huntley

The Groundings With My Brothers by Walter Rodney

after Walter Rodney, famous historian and founder of the Working People's Alliance in Guyana, who was assassinated in Georgetown in 1980. He was a friend of the Huntleys and used to stay with them when he was in London.

The first book published by Bogle-L'Ouverture was Rodney's *The Groundings with my Brothers*, an account of the major lectures he gave in Jamaica during 1968. Other notable titles were Linton Kwesi Johnson's *Dread Beat An' Blood*, Andrew Salkey's *Caribbean Folk Tales and Legends* and *The Proverbs of Guyana Explained* by Joyce Trotman. In 2009 they re-issued the groundbreaking book by Donald Hinds, *Journey to an Illusion: The West Indian in Britain*.

Both New Beacon and Bogle-L'Ouverture were active in anti-racist and other political activities and their bookshops became centres of organisation where meetings and cultural events took place. Issues such as education and police harassment were addressed. Campaigns were supported, such as the New Cross Fire demonstration, the supplementary school movement and the protest at the stoning to death of the Jamaican poet Mikey Smith.

Racist attacks on the bookshops were frequent, as Jessica Huntley recalls: "The National Front used to break windows. Then we got threatening calls. They give us seven days to move, and if we didn't get out, what's going to happen. We got calls from the Ku Klux Klan. They were everywhere. And, of course, we had a campaign against that and our poster was, 'We Will Not Be Terrorised Out of Existence'."

They collected a wealth of material relating to this historical period and this is now available to researchers. The Huntley Collections are stored in the London Metropolitan Archives.

"The National Front used to break windows. Then we got threatening calls. They give us seven days to move, and if we didn't get out, what's going to happen. We got calls from the Ku Klux Klan. They were everywhere. And, of course, we had a campaign against that and our poster was, 'We Will Not Be Terrorised Out of Existence'."

Chapter 13

The History of Caribbean Publishing in Britain:
Hansib Publications

"To a degree, well-known individuals (such as publisher Arif Ali, the late Rudy Narayan who as a barrister was a thorn to the judicial system, and Sir Shridath Sonny Ramphal) are lost to the Caribbean communities in Britain, because they are from Asian (East Indian in the Caribbean) backgrounds."
Harry Goulbourne *Caribbean Transnational Experience* 2002

"Arif's impact, like the majority of people who work within the black (as opposed to within the white) communities here in Britain, has been woefully overlooked."
Juliet Alexander 2009

"Arif's contributions have not yet received the many acknowledgements they deserve. I hope they will come and be an encouragement to him and the successors his achievements will certainly inspire."
Shridath Ramphal 2009

"Hansib is not only a publishing house: it's a movement." Paul Boateng

The 1970s saw the appearance of Arif Ali on the British publishing scene. In late 1970 he established Hansib Publications and in April 1971 the company launched *Westindian Digest*. This monthly magazine targeted Britain's West Indian community. It carried general news items and features from the Caribbean along with advertisements from mainly West Indian-owned businesses.

From this small beginning the business grew, so that in the 1980s, as Ionie Benjamin records in *The Black Press in Britain*: "The founder and owner of Hansib Publishing Company, Arif Ali controlled the largest number of newspaper and periodical titles in black publishing in Britain, regularly producing approximately five newspapers and periodicals in addition to books. At one time he owned the *West Indian Digest*, *African Times*, *Asian Times*, *Caribbean Times* and *Asian Digest*."

She goes on to quote his colleague Robert Govender who sees him as the "modern black pioneer in magazine and newspaper publishing, a title he has earned for over twenty years. Had Ali been born white, he would by now be on the same financial footing as Rupert Murdoch."

Similarly, in *A Century of Black Journalism in Britain*, Lionel Morrison writes: "Hansib Publications dominated the black media scene for the latter part of the 1970's and the first part of the 1980's. Hansib became one of the longest established Third World-oriented publishing houses in Britain and by that time was becoming the largest publishing house in Europe run by and for the visible minority communities."

Yet at the same time, a book entitled *Publishing for People*, funded by the Greater London Council and edited by Bob Baker and Neil Harvey, was produced in 1985. It was a directory of radical publishers, with over 200 entries. Whilst including New Beacon and Bogle-L'Ouverture, the authors make no mention of Hansib!

"Indo-Caribbean peoples in Britain have been overlooked by observers of all kinds - academics, the media, and the general public alike; they have been miscategorized in official statistics and in social perception; and they have been misunderstood by almost all they have come into contact with in this country."

Also in this century the political and intellectual contribution of Arif Ali to British cultural life is still often ignored. *The Oxford Companion to Black British History,* published in 2007, contains asection on black publishing, but only one short paragraph on Arif. A book on black activism and cultural politics, published in 2002, leaves him out completely, and there is not even a footnote on him in a collection of articles on West Indian intellectuals in Britain, which came out in 2003.

Another book, on the Caribbean diaspora, published in 2002, contains the sentence: "Caribbean communities in Britain have come to be defined in a manner that excludes people of Asian-Caribbean backgrounds." Yet, in a chapter on Caribbean publishers, the author includes one sentence on the *West Indian World* and its first editor Aubrey Baynes and over twenty pages on New Beacon and Bogle-L'Ouverture, but not one word on Arif Ali and Hansib Publications.

Steven Vertovec sees this as a general marginalisation of Indian Guyanese immigrants: "Indo-Caribbean peoples in Britain have been overlooked by observers of all kinds - academics, the media, and the general public alike; they have been miscategorized in official statistics and in social perception; and they have been misunderstood by almost all they have come into contact with in this country."

This gap between achievement and acknowledgement needs to be addressed and to begin the story we need to travel to Guyana where Arif Ali was born.

Chapter 14

Guyana

Amerindians

"But still they have their dances and at nights,
When the drums trouble the dark with rhythm
The violin takes a voice and patterns the air
And then the Indians find their tribal memories
Of victories and war and dim old journeys
That brought them from beyond the Behring Strait."
A. J. Seymour (1914-1989) *Over Guiana, clouds*

"A Region in Guiana, all Gold and Bounty."
Falstaff, in Shakespeare's *Merry Wives of Windsor*
1599

"and yet unspoil'd
Guiana, whose great Citie Geryons Sons
Call El Dorado."
John Milton *Paradise Lost* 1667

"El Dorado – that elusive place was never found.
The search for it cost many lives and terrible
suffering, particularly among the American natives."
John Hemming *The Search for El Dorado* 1978

"Gold was the watchword, gold the prize,
Gold's greedy ray shone in their eyes,
Gold was the search of weak and brave –
Their hope, their strife, their love, their grave."
Egbert Martin (Leo) 1883

Guyana is situated on the north coast of South America, with an area of about 83,000 square miles (almost the size of Britain), but historically and culturally it is part of the West Indies. It was first

Amerindian Family

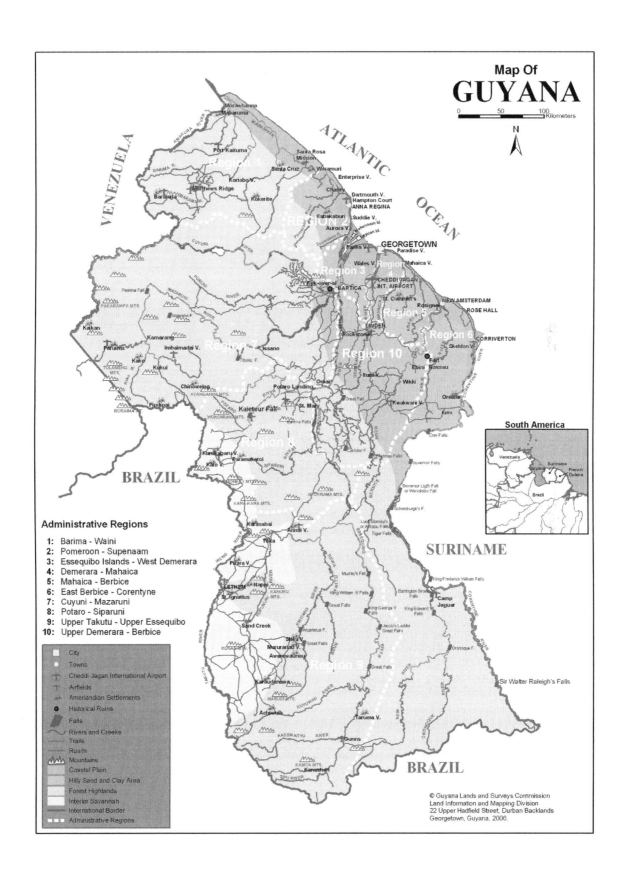

Map Of
GUYANA

Administrative Regions

1: Barima - Waini
2: Pomeroon - Supenaam
3: Essequibo Islands - West Demerara
4: Demerara - Mahaica
5: Mahaica - Berbice
6: East Berbice - Corentyne
7: Cuyuni - Mazaruni
8: Potaro - Siparuni
9: Upper Takutu - Upper Essequibo
10: Upper Demerara - Berbice

City
Towns
Cheddi Jagan International Airport
Airfields
Ameriandian Settlements
Historical Ruins
Falls
Rivers and Creeks
Trails
Roads
Mountains
Coastal Plain
Hilly Sand and Clay Area
Forest Highlands
Interior Savannah
International Border
Administrative Regions

© Guyana Lands and Surveys Commission
Land Information and Mapping Division
22 Upper Hadfield Street, Durban Backlands
Georgetown, Guyana. 2006.

South America

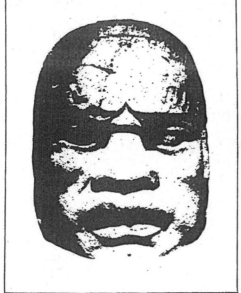

IVAN VAN SERTIMA

THEY CAME BEFORE COLUMBUS

RANDOM HOUSE NEW YORK

They Came Before Columbus by Ivan van Sertima

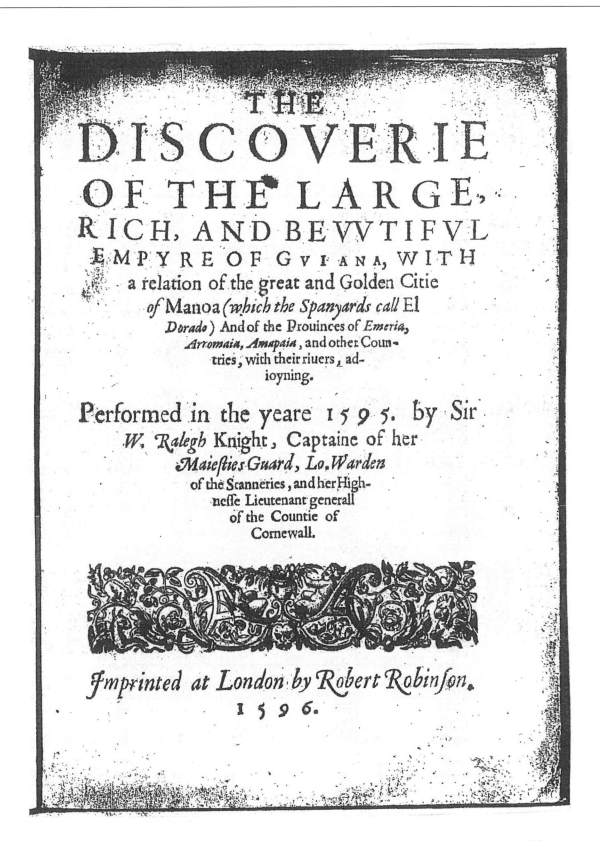

THE
DISCOVERIE
OF THE LARGE,
RICH, AND BEVVTIFVL
EMPYRE OF GVIANA, WITH
a relation of the great and Golden Citie
of Manoa (which the Spanyards call El
Dorado) And of the Prouinces of Emeria,
Arromaia, Amapaia, and other Coun-
tries, with their riuers, ad-
ioyning.

Performed in the yeare 1595. by Sir
W. Ralegh Knight, Captaine of her
Maiesties Guard, Lo. Warden
of the Scanneries, and her High-
nesse Lieutenant generall
of the Countie of
Cornewall.

Imprinted at London by Robert Robinson.
1596.

Front cover of Raleigh's Book *The Discoverie of the Large, Rich and Bewtiful Empyre of Guiana*

Walter Raleigh's route

Timehri rocks

Raleigh entering the Orinoco River

Raleigh with an Amerindian Chief

Arawak stilt house

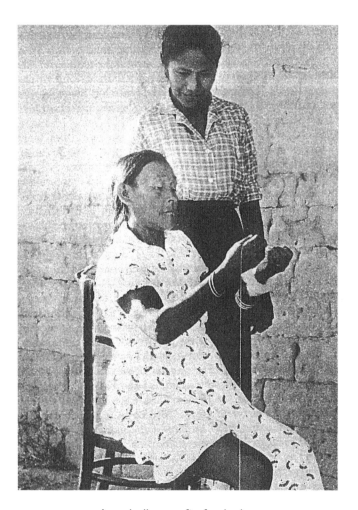

Amerindian craft of spinning

'discovered' by Europeans when Columbus travelled along the coast in 1498, on his third voyage. According to evidence amassed by the Guyanese historian, Ivan Van Sertima, however, Africans had already voyaged to this area many years before. When some of Columbus's crew landed, they saw "handkerchiefs of cotton very symmetrically woven and worked in colors like those brought from Guinea, from the rivers of Sierra Leone and no difference".

The first English explorer to arrive in the region was Walter Raleigh in 1595 and he wrote up his exploits in a book entitled *The Discoverie of the Large, Rich and Bewtiful Empyre of Guiana*, that went through three editions in 1596, which explains why it was known to Shakespeare. Around this time too the Dutch made a settlement on the coast.

But, of course, the area was already inhabited by Amerindians who had lived there for thousands of years. According to Denis Williams, the distinguished Guyanese artist and archaeologist, hunter/gatherers had arrived there 11,000 years ago, when Trinidad was still part of the mainland of South America. They developed agriculture about 7,000 years ago.

The Amerindians have literally left their mark on the land with their rock engravings (petroglyphs), depicting people, birds and animals such as monkeys, crocodiles and snakes. These carvings, called Timehri, are usually to be found near rivers, by cataracts and rapids. Aubrey Williams, the famous Guyanese artist, often uses these motifs in his painting.

Robert Schomburgk, the German scientific explorer who travelled throughout the country in the 19th century, asked the Taruma Indians about the sculptured rocks. They replied that "women had made them a long time ago". They were often used to record events, for instance fishing expeditions, and sometimes contain numbers. One petroglyph by the Kassikaityu River is an engraving of a fish trap. These traps were complex, made out of cane and fibre, and were of different kinds depending on the fish being caught.

The name Guiana comes from an Amerindian word for water, which is why the country is known as

Amerindians casting gold

El dorado being gilded with gold

'the land of many waters'. But the original inhabitants of the land, like the aborigines in Australia, have often been viewed as inferior. As one Amerindian resident of Moruca said in 2007: "People believe that Amerindians are at the bottom, every other race thinks they are above us and that is how it has always been."

Denis Williams, however, stresses their cultural importance, because of their traditions of adapting to the environment: "The earliest inhabitants of Guyana are our direct and valued ancestors irrespective of racial affiliation. Although our economies are linked today through trade to the economies of the rest of the world on a scale that would have been inconceivable a mere 300 years ago, there is no way in which we may ignore, without severe and sometimes costly loss, the permanent adaptive achievements of the earliest Guyanese. This is the element in our heritage which Europeans neither discovered nor destroyed."

Europeans came to Guyana in search of gold. After the Spanish had conquered the Incas in Peru and stolen their gold, the legend developed at the beginning of the 16th century that there lived in Guyana a king who was so rich that he covered his body in gold dust every day. Spaniards called him 'el dorado', the golden man. Each morning he would be anointed with gum or resin and then coated in powdered gold, as fine as ground salt.

Soon the term 'El Dorado' came to mean the city which was the capital of his empire. It even had a name, Manoa, and was said to be situated on Lake Parima in the interior of the country. Both these mythical places appeared on maps right up until the 18th century.

Rock carvings on the bank of the Rio Negro

Rock carvings by the Corentyne River

Chapter 15

Guyana

Slavery

The suffering and indignity of slavery.
Woodcut by artist Eddie Graham

"We have sea on this shore
Whole waves of foam groan out perpetually.
In the ships coming, in the black slaves dying
in the hot sun burning down –
We bear a mark no shower of tears can shift.
On the bed of the ocean bones alone remain
rolling like pebbles drowned in many years."
Martin Carter (1927-1997) *Fragment of Memory*

"Slaves moved 100 million tons of heavy, water-logged clay with shovel in hand, while enduring conditions of perpetual mud and water."
Walter Rodney (1942-1980)

"For a
re-awakening
Give ancient voices
release – from
the swamps of for-getfullness."
Marc Matthews *Chant Now 1987*

"In Guyana, for decades, puddings were covered with 'Golden Syrup' (Tate & Lyle) made in England from the Demerara sugar Caribbeans produced."
Aubrey Williams (1926-1990)

"born in Guyana, four score years ago
a creole mix
great grandson of a slave,
entangled in Scots kilts and Asian saris
slave master, indentured labourer
ancestral pawns on the
chess-board of colonial liaisons"
Cy Grant *an interior journey 2008*

Some gold was found, but the real wealth of Guyana was to be based on sugar. In 1621 a charter was issued to the Dutch West India Company to supply slaves from Africa, and eventually about 5,000 were imported every year. In the following years it was the labour of these Africans which built up the economy of the country. They cleared the land for the plantations, dug the drainage canals and ditches, and produced the sugar.

Slave in irons

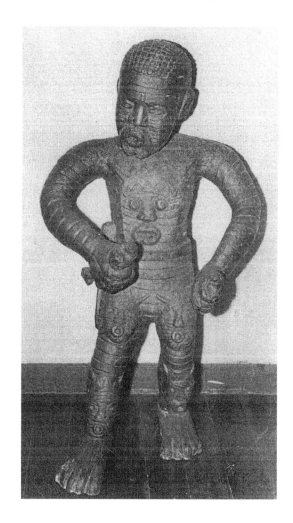

Statue of Cuffy, sculpted by Philip Moore

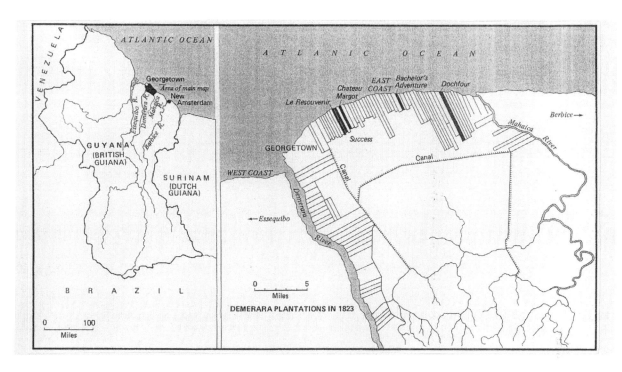

Demerara Plantations in 1823

They also rebelled. In 1763 a major slave uprising took place in Berbice, led by Cuffy and Accabre. It was not suppressed until almost a year later. Cuffy wanted to partition Berbice with the Dutch and so set up an independent state, as the Guyanese historian T. Anson Sancho points out: "They were the first slaves who from the midst of the filth and misery in which they lived dreamt of Independence." In his poem *The Ballad of 1763* he adds:

> "This diplomatic note which Cuffy sent
> Said whites might stay: the blacks would build a
>   nation
> But never more submit to white compulsion."

In 1823 an even greater slave rebellion took place in Demerara, involving about twelve thousand slaves from around sixty plantations. An English Methodist missionary, John Smith, was accused of instigating the revolt and he was tried by court-martial and condemned to death. The real leaders, however, were slaves – carpenters, boat captains and coopers, though many of them were also deacons or teachers in Smith's chapel.

John Smith

A gold prospector's camp

A sugar plantation

In the first few days of the rebellion a couple of white men were killed, but over 250 slaves were shot by the soldiers in the reprisals. Two of the leaders were father and son, Quamina, who was a carpenter and Jack Gladstone, a cooper, both from plantation Success where the revolt started. When Jack Gladstone was caught, he was banished to St Lucia, to prevent him becoming a martyr. Quamina was eventually found too and, when challenged, walked away, preferring to be shot than captured. In his pockets they found a knife and a bible. His body was hung up in chains on the road in front of Success.

In 1824 a book by Joshua Bryant was published in Guyana entitled *Account of an Insurrection of the Negro Slaves in the Colony of Demerara*. Bryant was an artist who had lived in the colony for 15 years and served in one of the regiments during the repression. The book gives a verbatim account of the court-martial of 72 "insurgent negroes". Thiry-two were executed, of whom ten were also beheaded. During this official trial, summary executions were still taking place on the plantations.

At their trial many of the slaves explained that they believed "freedom had come out for the slaves", but "it was withheld from us by our masters". (In fact some new laws had been sent out from Britain, prohibiting the flogging of slaves in the fields and the flogging of females.) Fourteen copies of Bryant's book were sent to Trinidad, 23 to Barbados and 28 to Jamaica, presumably to serve as a lesson.

An illustration in the book shows how the hangings and decapitations were used on the plantations to intimidate the slaves and deter them from further rebellion. It is worth reclaiming the pictures of these Guyanese heroes. The names of these plantations, such as Friendship and Success, present a horrific irony.

A pamphlet was published in London in 1824 entitled *Immediate, not Gradual Abolition*. It referred to the "sentences passed upon the insurgents of Demerara" and reported that "some were hung, others received 1,000 lashes and were condemned to be worked in chains during the residue of their lives".

John Smith died of pneumonia after being imprisoned in Georgetown for seven weeks, while

Lindor, a carpenter, on La Bonne Intention

Telemachus, teacher and head member of the church, and Jemmy on Bachelor's Adventure

Paul, on Friendship, and two heads displayed on New Orange Nassau

awaiting execution, before news of a reprieve by the British Government reached the colony. The reports of the event back in Britain had a dramatic response and helped the anti-slavery campaign, which finally succeeded ten years later.

Slaves also ran away into the interior and formed maroon communities. In *Shadows Round the Moon* Roy Heath recalls this period: "This dread of backland villages goes back to the time of slavery, when runaway slaves established villages in the interior, where the king's writ did not run. The only evidence of their presence would be the drumbeat that arrived on the wind at the dead of night, when their inhabitants lost their fear of marauding soldiers, who were frequently sent to destroy their crops and attack their villages."

Control of the colonies that made up Guyana (Essequibo, Demerara and Berbice) alternated between Dutch, French and British, until in 1803 Britain finally took them from the Dutch. In 1831 they were united into one country – British Guiana. After slavery was abolished on 1 August 1834, ex-slaves were forced to serve as apprentices, but many of them resisted this attempt to keep them in bondage. In Essequibo, on 9 August 1834, about 700 workers went on strike to protest against this apprenticeship. Its leader, Damon, was arrested and found guilty of rebellion. On 13 October he was hanged publicly in Georgetown on a special gallows facing what is now Parliament Building. Four others were sentenced to transportation to New South Wales and 31 to imprisonment and flogging.

After slave emancipation was finally achieved in 1838, former slaves set up their own co-operative villages and, as Christobel Hughes writes in *Guyana*: "Despite all the obstacles and lack of credit, the Africans found outlets for their creativity. They grasped education and became the professionals, teachers, village leaders, nurses, civil servants, doctors, lawyers, ministers of religion. They pioneered the mining and forest industries and agitated for reform of the political system."

Even in the late 20th century, however, the memory of slavery was passed on, as the Guyanese teacher and novelist, Beryl Gilroy, recalls in *Sunlight*

The seal of the colony –
'We give and demand in turn'.

Stamps issued in 1931 to celebrate the centenary of the union of the three colonies

Cutting the sugar cane

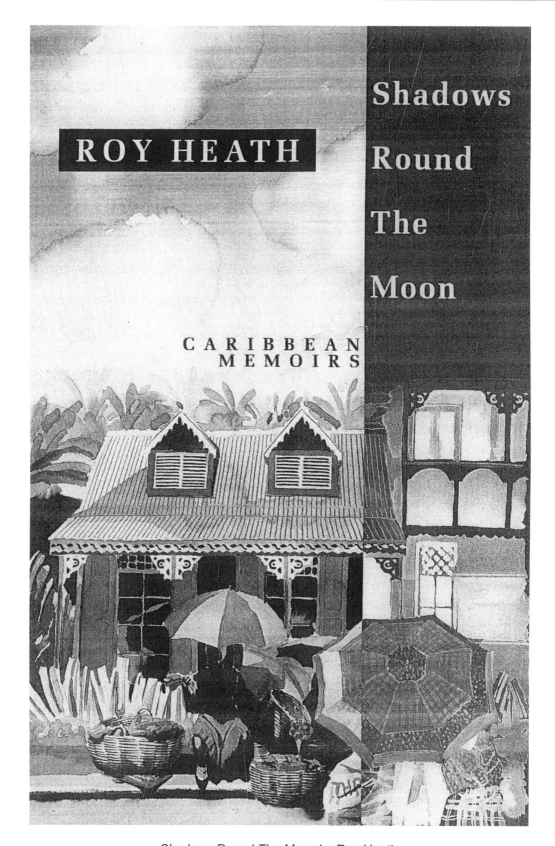

Shadows Round The Moon by Roy Heath

on Sweet Water: "My grandmother and my aunts served the cake and ginger beer that they forever made. They talked of times long gone, of slavery, and what it meant to those who experienced it, of injustices of all sorts, of exploitation, and of families who had been shattered by time. What a flow of history that evening was! Their speeches were interspersed with proverbs and other sayings from their forbears. I noted their regard for experience, which they all said no one could buy except from the market of life."

Beryl Gilroy

"This dread of backland villages goes back to the time of slavery, when runaway slaves established villages in the interior, where the king's writ did not run. The only evidence of their presence would be the drumbeat that arrived on the wind at the dead of night, when their inhabitants lost their fear of marauding soldiers, who were frequently sent to destroy their crops and attack their villages."

Chapter 16

Guyana

Indentured Labour

"Some came with dreams
Of milk and honey riches.
Others came, fleeing famine
And death."
Mahadai Das (1954-2003) *They Came in Ships*

"Man's dream of Utopia will never become a reality
as long as true love and justice remain as hard to find
as a mustard would be in the Gobi. We came with
high hopes that were shattered! This rich, green land
is no Eden. On promises we have worked as most of
us never worked before, haunted by our past,
immune to the present, and sometimes somewhat
afraid to think or even dream of another tomorrow."
Sheik Sadeek *Wind-Swept and Other Stories* 1980

"Cut, bind, cut and bind
Each leaf, each sheaf and knot.
A broken back, a tiring thigh,
A feverish groan, a heaving sigh,
No matter what, work or die!
That's the grass-cutter's lot."
Cyril Kanhai *The Grass-Cutter's Song* 1969

"One of the enduring myths about the Indians in
Guyana, and indeed in the entire Caribbean region,
is that they are a docile, conservative people
reluctant or incapable of initiating action to disrupt the
status quo. While such notions may apply to some
Indo-Guyanese who form part of the petty-
bourgeoisie, the militancy of Indian sugar workers
who constituted the largest single work force and the
most oppressed and exploited group after slavery

Indian woman reaping paddy

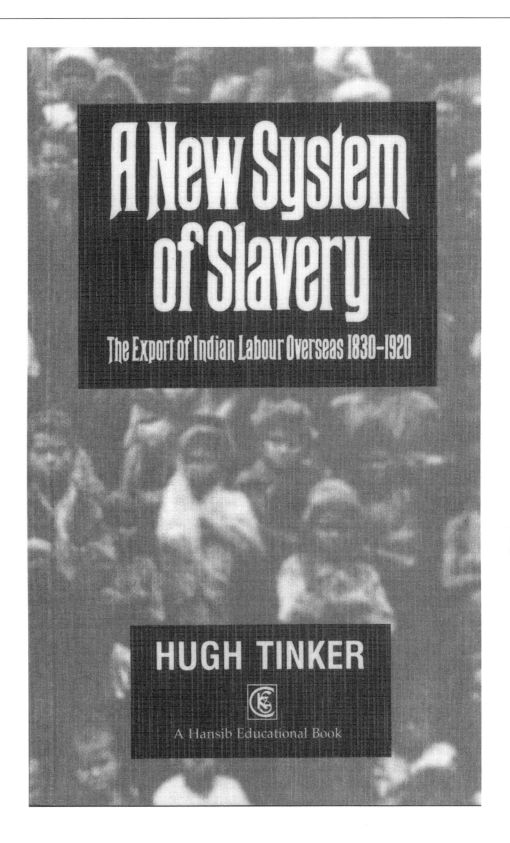

A New System of Slavery, Hansib Publications 1993

belied this." Basdeo Mangru *A History of East Indian Resistance on the Guyanese Sugar Estates* 1996

"I know the girls are coming,
For I hear the gently humming
Of choruses they're singing on their way;
I hear their saucepans jingling,
And their cutlasses a-tingling,
Which as their music instruments they play."
C. E. J. Ramcharitar-Lalla *The Weeding Gang* 1961

"Sugar was first crystallised from the cane plant in India. It is an irony of history that 2,500 years after that event Indians left their native land to travel thousands of miles across the world to pursue the manufacture which their far ancestors had first discovered." Ian McDonald *Tiger in the Stars*

In 1838 the exodus of ex-slaves from the sugar plantations began and, between that year and 1849, black plantation labour dropped from 80,000 to around 20,000. 1838 also saw the first immigrants from India arrive. Already in 1835 indentured Portuguese labourers had been brought in from Madeira and in the next few decades other workers would be imported from Africa, China and the West Indies, particularly Barbados. But by far the greatest number of indentured labourers came from India.

At first there was reluctance on the part of the British government to agree to this course of action, because it so closely resembled slavery. Lord John Russell, Secretary of State for the Colonies, stated on 15 February 1840: "I should be unwilling to adopt any measure to favour the transfer of labourers from British India to Guiana... I am not prepared to encounter the responsibility of a measure which may lead to a dreadful loss of life on the one hand, or, on the other, to a new system of slavery." So from 1838 to 1843, imported Indian labour was prohibited.

But eventually pressure from the planters, owing to the shortage of labour, led to its re-introduction and from that time, until the final abolition of imported indentured labour in 1917, nearly a quarter of a million Indians landed in the colony. They were

Indian indentured labourers disembarking at Port Georgetown, British Guiana. Circa early 20th century.

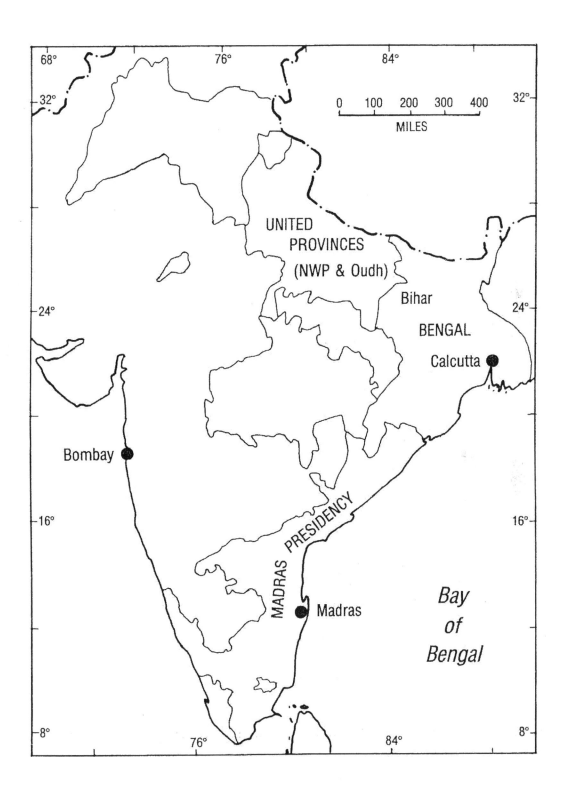

Main indentured recruiting areas in India

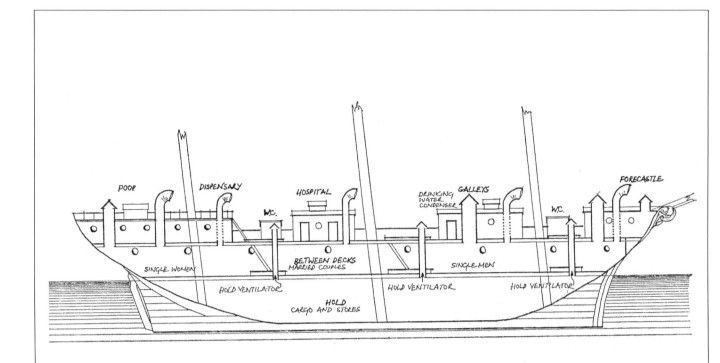

Cross-section of a ship carrying Indian indentured labourers

The export of Indian labourers to the Caribbean

Group of East Indians

Indian woman in the 1890s

"Those Indian hands whether in British Guiana or Trinidad have fed all of us. They are perhaps our only jewels of a true native thrift and industry."

George Lamming, *The West Indian People* 1966

On arrival the Indentured Indians were house in the old slave quarters

Indian forkmen and shovelmen in a sugar cane field

recruited by agents called 'arkatis', who were responsible for sending abroad about 5 million Indians in all. Those going to Guyana came mainly from Bengal in the north and Madras in the south. Most were Hindus, but about 15% were Muslims. By 1926 there were about 100 temples and mosques in Guyana. The Indians agreed to go because of famine and drought in India, but some were tricked into leaving and others even kidnapped.

Brij Lal, the Fijian historian, points out, however, that some of the women were actively seeking a new life: "The fact that women were prepared to part with a life of drudgery and unhappiness for the largely unknown would seem to me to suggest that many of them must have been individuals of remarkable independence, enterprise and self-respect. These were certainly the values they nurtured and lived by in the colonies."

The Guyanese historian Clem Seecharan agrees: "Many must have made a deliberate, considered decision to escape the sordid sameness, the tyranny of custom, and the social and material degradation in an impoverished caste-ridden society. They must have known that there could be no return for any woman who manifested such independence."

The voyage took three to four months, with everyone sleeping on blankets spread on the floor. Meals generally consisted of rice, flour, dhal, potatoes and pumpkins. The imbalance of men and women (about 40 women for every 100 men) led to the continual abuse of the women who emigrated to Guyana.

Clem Seecharan argues, however, that although over two-thirds of the women were not accompanied by any relatives "they took with them their ancient notion of the joint family as the basis of subsistence. Women were at the core of the joint family, crucial to its reconstruction as an instrument of cultural continuity." He also stresses the importance of religion (Hinduism and Islam) in resisting attempts to convert them to Christianity, while at the same time their common position as workers on the plantations weakened the strength of the caste system, hastening "the emergence of an infinitely more egalitarian Indian society".

Line drawing of an Indian indentured labourer, from a photograph of 1889

Life on a sugar plantation as seen through the eyes of an indentured labourer

The period of indenture settled at five years, but it could be extended to ten. Also fines and stoppages had to be worked off, so some workers were never able to get free. Some Indians claimed their free return passage, while some exchanged this right for two-acre plots of land to start rice farming. Only about one in five ever returned to the mother country.

For the majority, conditions were similar to slavery, as Walter Rodney pointed out: "The first Indian arrivals were treated in precisely the same manner as Africans under slavery." George Lamming confirms it: "There can be no question that Indian workers were now condemned to a history of humiliation almost indistinguishable from the memories of African slavery." He goes on to say how they lived in the deserted slave huts: "The tenement ranges or logies of the inherited 'nigger yard' were unventilated, the water supply was polluted and lavatory facilities non-existent."

In 1934 Jock Campbell went to Guyana to manage the family estates and was appalled by the living conditions of the East Indian cane cutters. Next to the tiny, dark, vermin-infested, earth-floored 'logies' on the Albion Estate in Essequibo was a clean, well-painted building. Jock asked who lived in the hovels. "Our coolies," replied James Bee, the estate manager. He then asked who lived in the smart-looking building. Bee said, "Oh! We keep our mules there." The naïve 22-year-old Jock asked: "Why don't you move your coolies to the mules' palace and put your mules in the hovels?" Bee exclaimed curtly: "Because it costs money to replace mules!"

According to Rodney: "It was in the interest of the planters to bring large numbers of Indians into Guyana, not because there was a shortage of labor, but to create a surplus of labor that one could use for lowering the wage rate." This is clear from two major strikes which took place against the planters'

Gandhi dressed as an indentured labourer with his two helpers, C. F. Andrews and W. W. Pearson, 1914

decision to cut wages. In 1842 the strike of largely black workers successfully reversed the decision, but in 1848, with growing numbers of Portuguese and Indian workers to draw from, the strike failed.

The policy of divide and rule is highlighted by Rodney: "Early in the history of indentureship, planters recognized the practical value of having a working population segmented racially; and they never lost sight of the opportunity of playing off the two principal races – by using one to put down any overt resistance by the other. J. E. Tinne forthrightly summed up this experience when he appeared before the West Indian Royal Commission. 'The two peoples do not intermix. That is, of course, one of our great safeties in the colony when there has been any rioting. If the negroes were troublesome every coolie on the estate would stand by one. If the coolies attacked me, I could with confidence trust my negro friends for keeping me from injury.'"

Rodney does not believe that this policy was completely successful, however, and he agrees with H. J. M. Hubbard who wrote in 1969: "It is by any standards a remarkable fact that in a competitive semi-feudal society such as British Guiana with restricted social and economic opportunities and less jobs than potential workers, very few serious physical inter-racial conflicts arose between the ethnic groups constituting the population."

In her novel *Timepiece*, Janice Shinebourne also puts forward a more positive approach to relations between African and Indian workers on the plantations: "Dutch plantations used to be situated along the river here, and slave rebellions were frequent. Those days were gone, but another layer of history had unfolded along the Canje river when indentured labourers had come to the area. The Afro-Guianese who remained were as close to their slave past as the Indo-Guianese to their indentured past. They still knew the names of the ships which had brought them to British Guiana. Africans and Indians shared each other's customs in a way that would be unthinkable elsewhere, and that was probably no longer possible after the race riots [1962-1964]."

Likewise Beryl Gilroy, who was born in Springlands, Berbice, in 1924, and who became London's first black head-teacher, recalls her multiracial primary school. In *Black Teacher*, published in 1976, she writes: "There we all were – children of six races – in quite enormous classes of about sixty to seventy children, and yet I can't remember a single day that we ever quarrelled about race. If there was ever any jealousy, it was socio-economic in origin."

At the time of the Royal Commission in 1897, about 90,000 people were employed in the sugar industry, more than a third of the country's population. Over 70,000 of those workers were of Indian origin. Indentured labourers were strictly controlled during working hours as Basdeo Mangru points out: "The law empowered a police officer or rural constable to apprehend an indentured labourer if found two miles away from his plantation without a 'pass' signed by the manager." He concludes that "slavery and indenture showed remarkable

A mixed group of immigrants

similarities". As Cheddi Jagan remarked: "Indentured immigrants were subjected to severe penalties. Their homes could be invaded at any time and they could be forced to work. Their place was either at work, in hospital or in jail."

In his book *The Coolie: His Rights and Wrongs*, published in 1871, British politician Edward Jenkins includes a woodcut "executed and brought to me in Georgetown by a clever Chinese immigrant, who had been a schoolmaster in his own country". The picture focuses on "a manager's house on its brick pillars". Bottom left is "a free Coolie driving his cattle" and bottom right a Chinese labourer being arrested by a rural constable. Above him is a group of Chinese with arms tied behind their backs and on the left of the picture a similar group of Indians. This is an "emblem of indentureship", as "they always speak of themselves as 'bound' when under indenture".

Jenkins explains the rest of the symbolism: "At the foot of the steps, on either side, is a Chinaman and a Coolie, from whose breasts two drivers are drawing blood with a knife, the life fluid being caught by boys in the swizzle-glasses of the colony. A boy is carrying the glasses up the steps to the attorney and the manager, who sit on the left of the verandah, and who are obviously fattening at the expense of the bound people below them. Behind, through a break in the wall, are represented the happy and healthy owners back in England. In the right-hand corner of the verandah is the pay-table, with the overseers discussing and arranging stoppages of wages."

Like the slaves before them, the indentured labourers rebelled against these conditions, as Brinsley Samaroo relates: "East Indian resistance to indentureship, often expressed in fashion similar to the African resistance to slavery, took the form of riots, strikes, desertion and murder of offending managers and overseers." Between 1885 and 1903 there were on average a dozen strikes each year, giving the lie to the myth of Indian docility."

In 1894 a remarkable Indian, Joseph Ruhomon, aged only 21, gave a lecture in St Leonard's Schoolroom in Georgetown, called 'India: The Progress of Her People at Home and Abroad, and how those in British Guiana may improve themselves'. He

"Life is business, it is real, it is earnest and does not consist in eating and drinking and fun and frolic and pleasure. You have got to be impressed with this tremendous fact that you are personally responsible for your own lives; see to it then that they are being properly spent and in such a way as would redound to your eternal credit. Do not remain idle whilst the hours are speedily fleeting away but rise up to the level of your grand opportunities."

In Black Teacher, published in 1976, she writes: "There we all were – children of six races – in quite enormous classes of about sixty to seventy children, and yet I can't remember a single day that we ever quarrelled about race. If there was ever any jealousy, it was socio-economic in origin."

celebrated the achievements of both Africans and Indians and stressed the importance of a "sound, broad and liberal education". He also saw women as "one of the most powerful of the forces at work in this 19th century, not only for the emancipation of her sex but in the common cause of humanity".

Above all, he emphasised the work ethic and called on fellow Indians to take responsibility for improving themselves: "Life is business, it is real, it is earnest and does not consist in eating and drinking and fun and frolic and pleasure. You have got to be impressed with this tremendous fact that you are personally responsible for your own lives; see to it then that they are being properly spent and in such a way as would redound to your eternal credit. Do not remain idle whilst the hours are speedily fleeting away but rise up to the level of your grand opportunities." When the lecture was published, it was the first publication by an Indian born in the Caribbean.

During the same period another Indian resisted oppression in a very outspoken way by continually writing letters to the press, protesting at the treatment of the workers. This was Bechu, an orphan from Calcutta, who had been educated there by Presbyterian missionaries. In 1897, for the Report of the West India Royal Commission, he was interviewed and asked how many hours he was employed. He replied: "I used to go to work at 6 o'clock in the morning, and come back at 6 o'clock in the evening. Frequently we have been kept back till 7 or 8 o'clock at night." He added that the time they had for meals was only "about an hour or half-an-hour". Ruhomon called Bechu "the invincible champion of his race".

The 1911 census revealed that East Indians formed the largest single ethnic group in Guyana. At this time, also, a protest was mounted in India against indentureship, led by the Indian National Congress under G. K Gokhale. When he died in 1915, Gandhi, who had just returned to India from South Africa, took up the leadership of the campaign, and in 1917 the system was halted throughout the British Empire. A few years later, on 15 April 1920, all outstanding indentures in Guyana were terminated.

In 1941 the Guyanese writer Edgar Mittelholzer wrote his first novel *Corentyne Thunder* about one of these Indian immigrants: "A tale we are about to tell of Ramgolall, the cow-minder, who lived on the Corentyne coast of British Guiana, the only British colony on the mainland of South America. Ramgolall was small in body and rather short and very thin. He was an East Indian who had arrived in British Guiana in 1898 as an immigrant indentured to a sugar estate. He had worked very hard. He had faithfully served out the period of his indenture, and now at sixty-three years of age he minded cows on the savannah of the Corentyne coast, his own lord and guide."

But even after the end of indentured labour, the Indian Guyanese were still at a disadvantage. In 1857 a pupil-teacher system was introduced for the African Guyanese, which meant that some of them could progress to become teachers and civil servants. On completion of primary school, an individual was qualified to become a pupil teacher and could proceed through several grades to become headmaster. This was often then a route to becoming a lawyer.

A law of 1876 made primary education compulsory for all, with 75% of the curriculum based on the bible. Enforcement, however, was practically non-existent, especially in the rural areas. The planters had no intention of encouraging children to go to school as it would deprive them of a valuable source of cheap labour. East Indian children were largely employed working in the fields, supplementing the family income. A report by the Government of India in 1914 commented on the lack of school attendance by Indian children: "Probably the principal cause of abstention is that children of 7 years and upwards can earn money by cutting grass, herding cattle, or doing light fieldwork."

In June 1904 this situation was formalised when the Governor, Sir James Swettenham, issued a circular exempting East Indian children from compulsory education during the first 10 years of their parents' residence in the colony. Also there was to be no penalty for parents who kept their children from school because they objected to the Christian religion being taught, or if they preferred not to send

Queen's College (1918-1951)

their daughters to school. In 1925 there were reported to be 22 estates employing children under 12 years of age on the sugar plantations or in the rice fields. They usually worked from 6am to 6pm and sometimes had to walk 8 miles to get to work

The school system was largely managed by Christian churches so Christian teachers were favoured, rather than Hindus or Muslims. As Cheddi Jagan records: "There were suggestions that if I wanted to become a teacher, I would have to become a Christian, and my parents would have none of this." In 1933, when the Swettenham Circular was finally withdrawn, East Indians made up only 6.6% of primary school teachers, although they were 41% of the population. At this time only 19% of East Indian children were enrolled in primary school.

Those who did attend school found themselves in overcrowded buildings in huge classes. The 1951-52 report on Primary Education Policy said it was not uncommon to find 800 children admitted to a school designed for 400. The report added: "Classes of 60 rapidly swell in number to 80 and 90; and classes over 90 are not uncommon."

As late as 1959, 298 of the 327 primary schools were owned and run by churches. It was the same situation with the secondary schools. Berbice High School, for example, which was attended by the famous Guyanese writers Edgar Mittelholzer and Jan Carew, was a Canadian mission school set up to convert students to Scottish Presbyterianism. Queen's College, where the politicians Cheddi Jagan and Forbes Burnham, novelist Wilson Harris and poet Martin Carter were educated, was founded in 1844 as a Church of England grammar school. In the 1950s Gordon Rohlehr, who became Professor of Literature at the University of the West Indies, studied there along with Walter Rodney. Bishop's College, the first teacher training institution in the country, started in 1851 as a theological seminary.

Things began to change when the People's Progressive Party won the election in 1957 and its leader Cheddi Jagan arranged for more schools to be built in rural areas, in an attempt to free the educational system from church control. By 1964, 41% of the teachers in the primary schools were East Indian, and by 1965 over 50% of doctors and lawyers were Indian.

Chapter 17

Guyana

Independence

*"See a prostrate people
Straighten its knee and stand erect
And stare dark eyes against the sun."*
A. J. Seymour *First of August* 1948

"If the Indo-Guyanese have to learn to recognise and appreciate the history of African sacrifice, and therefore the rights to power of the Afro-Guyanese, then equally the Afro-Guyanese must be educated as to the Indo-Guyanese role in the making of the Caribbean. Historic suffering and sacrifice (from which modern claims of inheritance to power are made) were not the prerogative of any one ethnic group. The Amerindian people, for instance, whose land we now occupy and squabble over, were nearly wiped out in two continents."
David Dabydeen 1987

*"I am coolie
You are black
So what?
Same germ
Same earth
Same nine months' embryo
Before we were born."*
Hemraj Muniram 1974

"Arguably the race and colour problem is the most bitter and divisive legacy we have inherited from our colonial past. In this sense the past definitely runs deep."
Alvin O. Thompson *The Haunting Past* 1997

People's Progressive Party, Hansib Publications 2007

Cabinet of People's Progressive Party Government in 1953. Left to Right: Ashton Chase (Labour and Commerce); Jainarine Singh (Local Government and Social Welfare); Cheddi Jagan (Premier, Agriculture, Forests, Lands and Mines; Janet Jagan (Deputy Speaker); Forbes Burnham (Education); Sydney King (Communications and Works); J.P. Lachmansingh (Health and Housing).

Cabinet of PPP Government in 1957. Left to Right seated: Janet Jagan (Labour, Health and Housing); Dennis Hedges (Chief Secretary); Sir Ralph Grey (Governor); Cheddi Jagan (Trade, Industry and Commerce); Brindley Benn (Community Development). Standing: Winston D. Wyatt (Asst. Clerk); Balram Singh Rai (National Resources); W.P. d'Andade (Financial Secretary); Ram Karran (Communicationsand Works); A.M. Austin (Attorney General); Arthur Abraham (Clerk).

Forbes Burnham, Prime Minister, and Cheddi Jagan, Leader of the Opposition

were some who ran one way.
were some who ran another way.
were some who did not run at all
were some who will not run again
Martin Carter *Black Friday* 1962

"We got six races of people
Livin' in dis lil country.
An' we always tellin' foreigners
How we don't got no racialism,
Or no prejudice
But we got a new fashion in de place now.
Black people changin' dey name
An' sayin' dey from Africa
Call deyself Kabomba or Kaluka.
East Indian people only goin' to see
East Indian pictures
Even though dey don't un'stan'
De language.
Chinese people only marryin'
Other Chinese people.
De Portuguese all leavin' de place
An' going to Canada
Dey say you got fo' be black or Indian
To live in Guyana.
Amerindian people hide away in de bush

An' only talking to dey own people.
An' European people feel
Dey better dan anybody else
Because dey ancestors come from Europe.
We all goin' back to we origins
An' until we can all get together
An' realize we's one race o' Guyanese
Dat's just how we going end up
Backward."
Evan Phillips *Going Back* 1974

The People's Progressive Party was formed in 1950 and united all those who wanted freedom from colonial rule. It was led by Cheddi Jagan, a dentist of Indian origin, and Forbes Burnham, a barrister of African origin. Under a new constitution in 1953 which provided internal self-government, the party won the election on a socialist platform of reform, but its power was only short-lived. The British and American governments feared a communist coup, so Britain sent in the army and declared a state of emergency. As Tom Driberg MP said at the time: "The reforms alarmed the Americans and would have inconvenienced the London financiers who dominate the life of British Guiana and exploit its people; so

Daily Chronicle, 24 June 1958

troops were sent, the Constitution suspended, and a 'red plot' rigged up."

In 1955 the party split into Jaganite and Burnhamite factions, which was to have disastrous long-term consequences. When elections were held again in 1957, Jagan's PPP won and Burnham's faction was renamed the People's National Congress. At fresh elections in 1961, Jagan was again returned to power, but there followed a period of social and racial unrest, fomented and financed by the CIA. Under pressure from President Kennedy, who feared another Cuba in his backyard, Britain intervened again and changed the voting system to one of proportional representation in order to disadvantage the PPP. It worked and in the 1964 election Burnham's PNC formed a coalition government with the United Force party, led by the businessman Peter D'Aguiar. The PPP had won 46% of the vote (24 seats), the PNC 40% (22 seats) and the UF 12% (7 seats).

On 26 May 1966 Guyana achieved independence, but the 1968 election was rigged to keep Burnham in power. Racial divisions were exacerbated. The PNC was said to have achieved 50% of the vote (although the black population at the time was 31%) and the PPP only 36% (despite the Indian population being 50%). As well as African Guyanese dominating the civil service and state bureaucracy, they also constituted 75% of the police and 90% of the army.

No wonder that the Burnham government felt threatened by the Working People's Alliance, led by Walter Rodney, the celebrated historian and political activist, who had returned from Tanzania in 1974, but had been denied a post at the university. Here was an African Guyanese arguing for racial unity. At political meetings they always arranged for both Indian and African speakers to be on the platform, challenging the divide-and-rule policy of the government. This is why Rodney was assassinated, on 13 June 1980.

In 1980 Burnham declared himself President, but the country was heading towards an economic crisis, with declining production of sugar, rice and bauxite. In August 1985 Burnham died and was succeeded by Desmond Hoyte. There was increased pressure for the restoration of democracy and in October 1992, under free and fair elections which were internationally supervised, Cheddi Jagan was returned to office after 28 years in the political wilderness.

In his first Address to the Nation, on 26 October 1992, he said: "To allay fears of racial/ethnic insecurity we propose, after consultations, to set up a Commission on Racial/Ethnic Equality. The United Nations has agreed to provide funding for this Commission." He went on to talk about "a comprehensive programme to bring about racial/ethnic amity and co-operation. Our educational system will be geared to break down prejudices and stereotypes and to provide opportunities for everyone to acquire qualifications for jobs. Laws will be made to make racial/ethnic incitement and unfair employment practices a criminal offence."

In 1997 Cheddi Jagan died and was succeeded by Sam Hinds. Then after elections in December of that year, Janet Jagan, wife of the late President, became the country's first woman President. When she resigned in 1999, Bharrat Jagdeo became President, at 35 years of age, making him the world's youngest Head of State. In 2001 Jagdeo won the election and again in 2006, with the PPP taking 54.6% of the vote and the PNC 34%.

Like Arif, many Guyanese have emigrated, mainly to the United States, Canada, Britain and the islands of the Caribbean. Another migrant, Clem Seecharan, who is now Professor of Caribbean History and Head of Caribbean Studies at London Metropolitan University, comments on this migration: "The population has, in fact declined from the early 1970s, when it was estimated at about 815,000; today it is under 800,000. In my village in the East Canje district of Berbice, over 80% of the original inhabitants have gone. Of 60 or 70 of us who completed secondary school, at Queen's College in 1968, I am not aware of a single one who still resides there."

"The reforms alarmed the Americans and would have inconvenienced the London financiers who dominate the life of British Guiana and exploit its people; so troops were sent, the Constitution suspended, and a 'red plot' rigged up."

Walter Rodney

Chapter 18

Arif Ali

Family and Childhood

"From the brutal pages
Of Guyana's history
Are the stories of heroines
Women of strength
And ironed will
Who stood
To fight
Illustrating life's record
With their precious blood."
Krishna Prasad *Our Heroines* 1978

"The sun sets on Leguan
As I lie listening to the clear brown waves
Washing-swishing-breaking in creamy foam
On the sands of Leguan."
Quentin Richmond *On the Sands of Leguan* 1961

"Leguan, look how you stand,
A sparkling gem lost
In the middle of the wide Essequibo!"
Rosetta Khalideen *Leguan* 1979

"As a child I worked this land half-naked,
Growing into patched, taken-in clothes.
It was one crop alongside another
For miles; tree-lined boundaries;
Paths waving deep into shrubbery
Breaking onto clearings, far as the eye."
Fred D'Aguiar *Guyanese Days* 1985

Arif Ali was born on 13 March 1935 in Danielstown, on the Essequibo coast. He is one of seven children. He comes from a business family who owned a rice mill

Arif's mother, Nasibun "Sibby" Ali

Arif returns to his old primary school St Lawrence at Hampton Court, *West Indian World* 20 February 1976

at Hampton Court where Arif spent his early years. They also owned a coconut estate at Better Hope and various other businesses such as a general store at Danielstown, fishing boats, cattle and a timber grant at Pickersgill on the Pomeroon river. Outside the mill was a large area of concrete where the padi was dried after being parboiled and the coconuts dried for copra. It was here that Arif played cricket and marbles, and learnt to ride donkeys.

One of his grandparents, his father's mother Ulphat, was born in Guyana. Two grandparents came as indentured labourers from India: his paternal grandfather Siad Amjadally and maternal grandmother Sayeda Bee. His mother's father Mirza Wali Beg came to Guyana as a businessman. In an interview in 1984 Arif talked about his grandfather Amjadally: "A coolie is someone whose grandparents came out of indentured labour in Guyana, Trinidad and some of the other smaller islands. That means those people will either be of Chinese background or Indian background from the Indian subcontinent, but of course the word is used in Asia widely: the coolies are the people who labour. But in Guyana, just as the people of African background came out of slavery, so did my grandparents. My grandfather came from India at sixteen. He was indentured and he used to get whipped at a place they call in Danielstown 'Nigger Yard'. So when people talk about slavery and if they have the opportunity of meeting such a man, as I have met my grandfather, they will understand that there was much similarity between slavery and indentured labour."

Arif has good memories of his primary school St Lawrence Methodist at Hampton Court where the pupils were mainly East Indians. He showed early promise and recalls coming home one day, when he was about seven years old, to tell his mother that he had come top of the class. He liked reading and listening to stories and fables read by his teachers.

His family were Muslims and his grandfather Amjadally was a moulvi (priest) at the Better Hope and Danielstown mosque. Their immediate neighbours on one side were the Rajans (Hindus) and on the other an African Guyanese lady who worked for Arif's family. She was addressed as Cousin Ella and lived with her daughter Tun and grandson Ovid who was always at Arif's home.

Arif thinks that his respect for people of all classes, creeds and religions may have derived from the liberalism of his parents, especially his mother. They had a live-in help Patangee, who was of Hindu background, and she took daily care of the children and the home. It was Patangee or Chan Didi, as she was later known, who was bathing baby Arif when he jumped out of the bathing receptacle and fell down the stairs. The scar on Arif's left cheek is still there! He says: "Cousin Ella and Chan Didi were not blood family, but were addressed and treated as such, even to the point of administering discipline."

Arif remembers Hampton Court as being a busy home with visitors and much laughter in the evenings. During the milling season it was like a market place, with people, donkey carts, dray carts and endless bags of rice and padi constantly on the move. As a young child Arif told his mother that he was the 'Feesikeebo Star', which was meant to be 'Essequibo Star', and to this day his brothers and sisters sometimes call him 'Star'. His eldest brother Zahid, who sadly died in 2009, never called him anything else but 'Star'! His mother Nasibun (Sibby), on the other hand, always called him Aro and much to the disgust sometimes of his siblings, would say, "Where is my golden Aro?"

On his return from the estate at Better Hope, Arif's grandfather, Siad Amjadally, had to pass Hampton Court to get back to Danielstown. Arif remembers him calling from the road, sitting in a donkey cart. Even though the family had several cars, Amjadally always travelled by donkey cart. When Arif went to meet him, his grandfather always told him that the fruits he had brought, water melon, mangoes or sugar cane, were for him alone. Arif says, "I was a greedy kid and took Dada's word as gospel. When he drove away I refused to share

> "Love, education and initiating the love of God to their fellowmen come to mind when one reflects on the Maria's Delight Jamaat that is 100 years old. The Masjid was initially founded by brother Amjad Ally, formerly of Danielstown Village, Essequibo Coast in 1906, at Better Hope. Mr Ally who owned the estate on which the first place of worship stood at Better Hope, constructed the wooden building. In 1910, the Masjid was relocated to Maria's Delight."
>
> Yannason Duncan, *Kaieteur News*, Guyana, 18 April 2010.

anything with anyone!" His mother told him how mischievous his grandfather was and that Arif had undoubtedly inherited some of his traits!

Arif's father Hanif lost three brothers in their early years and his grandfather also died in 1939. The entire family business was handled by his grandfather and their wealth evaporated within a short period. The Second World War brought economic difficulties, as they could not get spare parts for the Dutch Peters engine that was used in the rice mill. Arif and his brother Kashiff helped to keep the engine going in very dangerous conditions, but eventually the business was sold. In 1944 they all moved to Leguan, an island in the mouth of the river Essequibo, where his mother's side of the family owned a 500-acre rice estate.

Leguan

Arif was then nine years old. He remembers the sadness at leaving the familiar environment, family and friends, and one particular incident still lingers in his memory. His father insisted on taking their horse 'Lady Grey', but travelling from the Essequibo coast to Leguan entailed a lengthy sea journey and there were moving restrictions on animals. Eventually, however, 'Lady Grey' arrived and all the family were pleased.

Arif's grandmother Seyada Bee had died in 1943 and his mother attended the funeral in Leguan. She

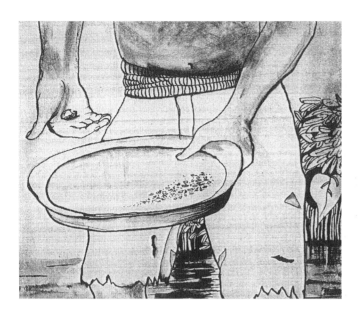

Pork-knocker, drawn by Aubrey Williams for Jan Carew's novel *Black Midas*

was told that a few acres of land was her inheritance, so this probably inspired the move to Leguan, which Arif's father was not in favour of. On arrival in Leguan, however, the land allocated to Nasibun Mirza Ali was either sold or taken.

Four of her brothers and three sisters inherited the spoils of the 500 acres, but Arif's mother and her younger sister Zabida got nothing. His mother used to explain this non-inheritance by saying that her family thought she had married well and was fine and that her sister Zabida had also married a well-off book-keeper and estate manager, Abdool Jabbar.

Arif recalls: "I would sometimes reflect that maybe my father's aloofness to my mother's family was based on the embarrassment he felt at having to come to Leguan, or maybe the fact of the non-availability of her inheritance."

They had some difficult months staying with his mother's sisters: first with Hasibun at the family home in Amsterdam, where his mother was born; then at Endeavour, half a mile away, with Afrose; then with Jaitoon at Windsor Forest, West Bank Demerara.

These were somewhat trying days, but not unhappy, as they gave the Ali children an opportunity to live with their first cousins from their mother's side, as Arif explains: "That relationship has continued with our cousins from my mother's side, and with the closeness we already had with the cousins from my father's side, my sisters and brothers often reflect that some of our best friends are our cousins and their families."

Arif's parents eventually bought a house at Belfield in Leguan. The property was described as 'Doctor Yard' and it had a grave in front of it. The house was not as big as the one at Hampton Court, but the land around it brought back fond memories of the Amjadally's home in Danielstown where Arif was born, was circumcised and where he spent some marvellous times with his father's family.

At Hampton Court there were no fruit trees, except for the coconut trees at the back of the rice mill. Arif describes the contrast with Belfield: "'Doctor Yard' had about one and a half acres of land, next to the Maryville Canadian Mission School. The house overlooked the Essequibo River and was only a stone's throw from the sea-dam. There was an abundance of fruit trees: about six mangoes of several varieties, guava, cashew, custard apples, sugar apple, sapodilla, papaw, lemon, lime, coconut, tamarind and a pineapple grove – the sourest I have ever tasted! Belfield also gave a permanent home to 'Lady Grey', who by this time had a foal. 'Lady Grey' died at Belfield and we buried her under the sapodilla tree where she had died."

The family spent about six years in Leguan. Arif's father had a government contract to supply transportation by car for officials and dignitaries, which included the weekly visit by the off-island based doctor. Arif remembers the British Governor of Guyana visiting and his sister Khalda placing a garland over his head when he arrived by sea-plane. His father's car was used to take the Governor around. After the Governor left, his father was taking Arif, his brother Kashiff and sister Khalda home when the car had an accident and went off the road. Fortunately none of them were injured.

Arif often thinks of his early teenage years spent in Leguan. He recalls with much fondness his Auntie Zabida, his cousins Shamie and Liala, and their father Abdool Jabbar: "The Jabbar family were always very helpful to the Alis."

Cousins and their families at a family get-together at Arif's home in Hertfordshire

At school, Arif recalls the two headmasters at Maryville Canadian Mission: "Mr Samaroo and Mr Yaw, who was the first African Guyanese to be appointed head-teacher at the school. Mr Yaw can be credited with some of the early influences on my thinking. He had studied in the United States and would mention in passing black people's right to liberty and fairness. He encouraged me to read and to take part in the school's annual harvest concert. One year I was involved in solo singing, group singing, had to read a poem about a doctor and was in the main school play about the sacrificial lamb. Mr J. T. Yaw described me to my older brother Kashiff as 'crazy, but brilliant'! I also remember the school sports day between the five schools on the island and the cricket matches on the school playground which was situated between our home and the school."

Much of Arif's leisure time was spent climbing up trees or on the beach, just in front of the house, catching fish or shrimps, or playing marbles on tagwa for broken china pieces or buttons. They had a dog called Rex and Arif remembers Rex's encounter with a porcupine when he and his brothers had to pull out the quills with pliers from the frisky dog's mouth! Arif also often organised picnics for his sister Khalda and cousin Liala.

His best friend in Leguan was Nazir Khan, who sadly died in January 2010: "Nazir was exactly one year to the day older than me and as a fourteen-month old baby was found in his cot with his head stuck between the bars! His family were the victims in a mass murder which took place on 6 May 1935."

Abdool Rahman Khan, Nazir's grandfather and owner of the Maryville estate, Nazir's mother and five other members of the family and staff were murdered. The 'Leguan Mass Murder', as it was known, was not surpassed until the early sixties when politicians, with the help of the American CIA, inspired the killing of hundreds of Guyanese, followed later on 18 November 1978 by the Jonestown massacre when 918 people died.

Arif's older brothers Zahid and Kashiff attended the People's Academy, a high school founded by a former teacher Victor Outarsingh, and his sister Khalda attended the primary school at Endeavour, where the high school was. The family had two cars: a Model T Ford with running boards and what his father described as a gas guzzler, the V8 Ford. There were two drivers: Sammy who had worked with his grandfather in Essequibo and now lived with them in Leguan, and Jeff from Success who lived most of the time at Belfield.

Family friends included George Jhagroo, head-teacher of Endeavour School, and A. R. Khan, the Government Sanitary Inspector of Leguan. Both men, and other friends, were regular guests at the Ali's home. There was much eating and drinking, especially the 'swank' which the boys made with limes, lemons, water and Demerara brown sugar. Even at home the children's education continued because of the background and conversation of the visitors: "A. R. Khan, Uncle Bert to the family, taught me the Irish national anthem, when I was fourteen. After that, with a little persuasion from my father, every visitor to the home had the discomfort of having to listen to my rendition in a girlish voice of 'Oh Danny Boy'!"

In 1950 the family left Leguan for Georgetown, after Arif's father lost the Government contract to what was then described as a "lower mileage bid". Arif had already completed a year in standard 6, but could not take the school leaving examination because he was not yet sixteen. Discussions between Mr Yaw and Arif's parents concluded with the idea that he could stay with his Auntie Zabida for the year while the family moved to Georgetown.

The family moved to Georgetown before the Belfield sale was completed. Arif was not happy with this arrangement, as on the way to school he was expected to check out that all was well at Belfield. He found out that people were sleeping in the house and told his aunt. This was the beginning of Arif's successful campaign, which to this day causes much laughter among his siblings, to join his family in Georgetown.

Georgetown

In Georgetown, after several attempts to rent adequate affordable premises, the family eventually settled down at 10 Shell Road in Kitty: "a two-storey large white house with a four foot high bottom area".

Arif attended Bedford Methodist School near Bourda market to take his school leaving examination, but he found school boring and was also teased on account of his country accent and because he was the only Indian in the class. He skipped school for several weeks, familiarising himself with the Botanical Gardens, Promenade Gardens, Georgetown library and, when he had the 8 cents, a film matinee.

The school eventually informed his parents. Arif got a hiding, but he bluntly refused to go back, even though his teacher Mrs Best sent a message to say he could still pass the school leaving examination, despite being away for some time. However Arif refused to take the examination out of sheer embarrassment.

A few weeks later the family had a visit from a representative from Tutorial High School in Georgetown to inform his parents that he had been offered a part scholarship, tuition and books, if they supplied the uniform. Unknown to his parents, Arif had taken the examination one Saturday morning, some weeks earlier, and was partly successful. This caused Arif some embarrassment as his parents informed the gentleman that, only a few weeks earlier, he had refused to go to school – yet he still went to take the examination!

After some laughter and a couple of slaps on his face, Arif refused to have anything to do with formal education, scholarship or no scholarship. Instead he got a job at Jaikaran's Drug Store in Regent Street. At the same time, without his parents' knowledge, he attended Mr Alexander's evening classes in Third Street, studying English, Maths, History and Latin. The other pupils were all taking extra classes and Arif found he was able to hold his own and even assist the younger pupils.

Arif's reading expanded even more by spending hours in Georgetown library, a habit he had acquired when he used to skip school. But now he was not questioned about why he was there when he should have been in school! He read Disraeli's *Sybil* and Tolstoy's *War and Peace*.

He was also introduced to British history by the son of a family friend. His name was Ayube McDoon, a student at Queen's College, who later became a lawyer and politician. Arif learnt about British prime ministers such as Pitt, Peel, Disraeli and Gladstone. He also read about Napoleon and the French Revolution, Baden Powell and scores of other topics. He developed an insatiable appetite for knowledge and read anything he could lay his hands on, including comic books: "My father told my mother that he once found me reading all the labels on the medicine bottles!"

Arif remembers that his books were scattered all over the house, many hidden away under his bed, most of which were library books. One day, on his return home, his mother greeted him at the door. She asked him: "Do you notice anything?" He replied, "No." She said, "Look over there." Lo and behold his first book cupboard which his father had built for him.

Arif's leisure time was taken up with cricket, volley ball and table tennis which was played on the large dining table which his elder brother Kashiff, who was an apprentice joiner, had built. He also became interested in scouting and eventually founded Troop 41, with the support of the Muslim Youth Organisation. His brother Kashiff later founded another scout group, with the support of the Indian Youth Organisation.

Their home became a headquarters for scouting activities with full support from all the family. The house was always filled with visitors and several cousins from all over Guyana used to stay there while in Georgetown. In 1955 Arif, an underage scout master, was selected, with fifteen other scouts, to go to Trinidad to meet Princess Margaret, who was not coming to Guyana because of the strained political situation.

Like most Guyanese, Arif became politically conscious around the time of the 1953 election when Guyana had become a unified political force, electing the People's Progressive Party, with Cheddi Jagan and Forbes Burnham as it leaders. The Waddington constitution was suspended eight months later and Guyana became a military occupied territory, with the arrival of The Royal Welsh Fusiliers, The Argyll and Sutherland Highlanders and the Black Watch.

Arif with Mrs Best, his retired former class teacher at Bedford Methodist, Georgetown 2008.

Arif also became interested in the co-operative movement and learnt about its English origins in Rochdale, Lancashire, in 1844, when members were first paid a dividend on their purchases. Co-operatives existed in different forms before this time, however, both in England and Guyana. After final emancipation in1838, former slaves established 'co-operative villages', pooling resources and organising themselves democratically. The Guyanese historian T. Anson Sancho claims that "they started the most remarkable co-operative movement in the history of the world". He adds: "Our history reveals that the first collective farms were laid out not in Russia but in Guyana at the time." It is also a continuation of the Amerindian co-operative economy. This living tradition is what drew Arif to socialism.

In the 1950s, however, most of the sugar plantations were owned by a family company called Booker, so much so that the country was often

Arif (centre) as Scoutmaster (Troop 41) in Guyana, 1955

referred to as 'Booker's Guiana'. Between 1952 and 1967, the chairman of the company was Jock Campbell, who strangely enough was a Fabian socialist with the belief, "People are more important than ships, shops and sugar estates." (Later he founded the Booker prize for literature.) He set about reforming and modernising the business.

Arif wanted some practical knowledge of the cooperative movement, so he volunteered his services on Saturdays at the co-op store at Brickham police station, the first of its kind in Guyana. Here he gained valuable information about the working of the store and its membership.

In 1956 the Guyana Sugar Producers Association, under the leadership of Arthur Hemstock, who came from the UK, decided to experiment with cooperatives and they opened their first store at Blairmont Estate on the west coast of Berbice. Their second shop was earmarked for Diamond Estate in East Bank Demerara.

Along with 22 other candidates, Arif applied for the manager's job. He was short-listed with one other, who was offered the job, but turned it down because the salary was not sufficient. Arif was then offered the job

and was told that his knowledge and enthusiasm about the movement was superior to all the other applicants. The only reason he was second choice was because he was too young at twenty-one. Arif worked with the Diamond Co-op for six months, during which time he assisted with the opening of Albion Estate Co-op in the Corentyne.

In 1957 Arif was very active in the election campaign, when Guyana returned to a limited democracy. But on 12 August, the day of the election, he left Guyana with his friend Sulaiman Khan. Earlier that year, in February, his elder brother had gone to England to study and asked Arif if he wanted to come and join him. This was to be a momentous decision. He decided to go. His family thought he would come back to be prime minister!

They flew to Trinidad, staying there for a week with friends Arif had made during his previous visits. Then they sailed on the SS Venezuela, via Tenerife and Barcelona, finally arriving at Genoa. From there, along with hundreds of other immigrants, they travelled to Calais, crossing the Channel to Dover, and taking the train to Victoria Station in London, arriving on the 3 September 1957.

Chapter 19

Arif Ali

Coming to England

"Mahaica was a womb out of which I had been wrenched and I did not want to return to it. Books had made me divided in myself and I knew I would remain that way as long as I lived. On the one hand, the language of books had chalked itself on the slate of my mind and, on the other, the sun was in my blood, the swamp and river, my mother, the amber sea, the savannahs, the memory of surf and wind closer to me than the smell of my sweat."
Jan Carew *Black Midas* 1958

"Looking at things in general life really hard for the boys in London. This is a lonely miserable city, if it was that we didn't get together now and then to talk about things back home, we would suffer like hell. Here is not like home where you have friends all about. In the beginning you would think that is a good thing, that nobody minding your business, but after a while you want to get in company, you want to go to somebody house and eat a meal, you want to go on excursion to the sea, you want to go and play football and cricket. Nobody in London does really accept you. They tolerate you, yes, but you can't go in their house and eat or sit down and talk. It ain't have no sort of family life for us here."
Sam Selvon *The Lonely Londoners* 1956

"'No Children!
No Irish!
No dogs!
No coloureds!'
That's what the notices read!"
Clarence C. Thompson *My Mother Country* 1973

West Indian immigrants arriving at Paddington Station, 9 April 1956

Outside a Labour Exchange, *Going To Britain?*, 1959

"In England West Indians do all kinds of work – on the railways as linesmen, porters, firemen, guards, and on the buses as conductors and drivers; in the factories, as postmen and as garbage collectors or street cleaners, but to get into any of these jobs you have to be able to read and write. If you can't read or write you will find it almost impossible to get work."
David Muirhead *Going to Britain?* 1959

Arif arrived at Victoria Station with only one penny in his pocket, knowing his brother was living in north London! He was one of over 7,000 Guyanese (1.3% of the population) who emigrated to Britain between 1955 and 1961. He had become part of what Louise Bennett called "colonisation in reverse", though like many West Indians at the time, he intended on going back after four or five years. The year he arrived, a fellow-Guyanese, Cy Grant, was singing the news calypso-style on the BBC television programme *Tonight*.

His first attempt to find work was at the co-op shop in Wood Green, where he imagined he could use his experience gained in Guyana, but, as he says, "They didn't want to know!" Not to be put off, he reflected that many people he had read about had started out in life doing menial jobs and, as he was not averse to hard work, eventually got a job as a porter at Coppetts Wood Isolation Hospital.

This involved a variety of tasks, such as moving dead bodies, stoking the boilers and working in the laundry. Arif was the only non-white person working as a porter and there was only one black nurse. Most of the domestic workers in the kitchen were Italian, Spanish and other European workers on six- month contracts, with some Swiss and German girls training as nurses. Arif recalls the experience: "Working with people of so many different backgrounds was itself an education. Those eighteen months gave me an insight into discrimination and racism. I was aware of the jokes made at my expense, so I began to inform them of their shortcomings and would give as good as I got! Eventually they asked me to clarify points about history and other subjects and I began to command respect."

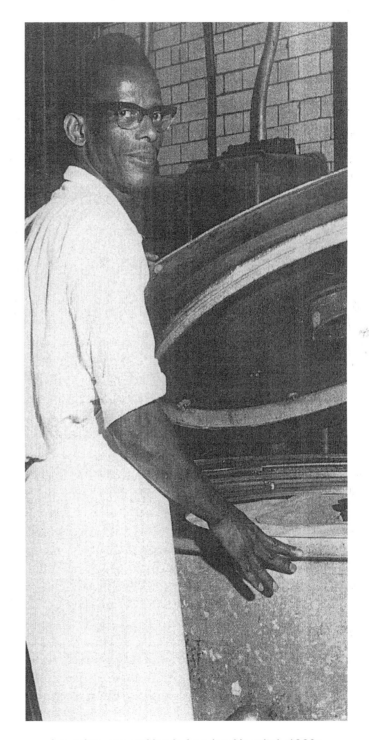

Laundryman working in London Hospital, 1960s

Meanwhile he carried on with his voracious reading. At Muswell Hill Library you were allowed to take out 4 books at a time, but somehow Arif managed to persuade the librarian to let him keep 11 or 12! He read more history, about the Chartists and the Co-operative movement, Disraeli and Lenin. Once he asked for Hitler's *Mein Kampf* and was surprised when the librarian asked him if he could read German. He then realised he would need the English version!

Working in the hospital was to change his life because there, in 1958, he met a seventeen-year-old nurse called Pamela and fell in love. Three months later, on 31 January, 1959, they got married. Arif did not tell his parents, though he did write to them a few days before the wedding saying that when they received the letter he would already be wed.

Arif tells the story of how Pamela told her grandmother: "She went to the phone box and called her, putting the phone a little bit to my ear and this is what I heard – 'Pammy, darling, is he dark, is he very dark?' Pam said, 'I'm going to bring him home.' When I went, they took to me and there was no friction, even though previously Pamela had not mixed with anyone of a non-white background. They were more receptive to me than my family was to Pamela."

Back in Guyana Arif's parents were not too pleased and when they received the wedding photos his grandmother threw them across the floor. His parents eventually moved to Canada and ten years later when Arif took the family to visit, his parents fell in love with them and all was well.

After getting married he decided to leave his porter's job and look for better pay. He became one of the 4,000 West Indians who joined London's transport system between 1955 and 1961. He started as a bus conductor and after six months passed his test to be a bus driver.

A BBC publication, called *Going to Britain?*, based on a series of broadcasts to the West Indies in 1959, advised people on the significance of the tea-break in British culture: "You will soon find out how important it is to break for tea, particularly during the winter months when it is very cold. Tea not only keeps you warm but is the most popular drink in Britain. Drink

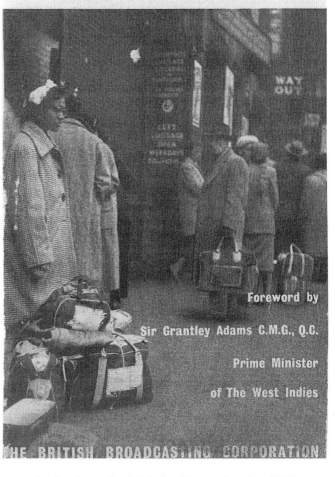

Advice from the BBC Caribbean Service 1959

your 'cup of char' as your cup of tea is sometimes called, with your work mates."

There was no advice, however, on what happened to Arif at tea-break, so he had to think quickly on his feet. In the canteen they all had to put two shillings in the kitty for tea, but Arif was asked for two shillings and sixpence. When he queried this, he was told that the sixpence was for sugar. He replied that he will not take sugar, and that was when he gave up taking sugar in his tea for good!

One incident while working as a bus driver led Arif to reflect some years later when he was interviewed:

Former members of the pop group 'In-Betweens' 1967. Mike Bakridan (drummer), Arif (Manager), Carmen Samad (lead singer), Alan Johnson (lead guitar), Ken Bakridan (rhythm guitar) at a dinner hosted by Alan Johnson at the House of Commons 2008.

Arif: One day somebody punched me on my mouth and I had to go to hospital. And he didn't call me a brown bastard because of my Asiatic background. He didn't call me anything else but a black bastard. And I never forgot that. My conductor was standing there. He said, 'But, Rif, you are not black', and that idea then came up to me that what people describe you as, the time has come for you to accept that, and since that time, ten years before I decided to launch my publications, I have been thinking and using that sort of idea.

Interviewer: Are you saying that it took coming to this country to realise that you were black?

Arif: Yes. In Guyana you couldn't call me black. In Guyana I am an Indian or a coolie.

Winston James, the Jamaican historian, comments on this event: "It is not, strictly speaking, a case of his realising on arrival in this country that he was black; it would be more accurate to say that he became black through his experiences in a racist Britain – the wider society defined him as black and he felt, as he explained, that it was sensible for him to embrace the new definition of himself, his new identity."

Arif was advised to take his attacker to court, but even now he is philosophical about the situation. His motto is not to spend time getting even: "Don't get even, get on!"

Another example of racism occurred when he put in for an inspector's job. At the interview he was told that he had passed all the tests, but he never got promoted: "I later learnt that this was because it was thought that the passengers would not accept a West Indian as someone who could inspect their tickets on the bus and that white bus drivers and conductors may not be receptive to a black inspector." A much more aggressive incident was to

Arif with Harold Wilson and Joe Haines, Jamaica 1975

my knowledge I was the first and only non-white sports secretary among the thirty at London Transport, yet I was refused promotion because of my skin colour!"

In 1963 Arif left the buses and moved his family out of London to Hertfordshire. Here he became a salesman, selling tea-bags, pickles and Collins encyclopaedias! He also worked as an assistant accountant for a building firm and dabbled in the music business, managing several pop groups. One of his groups was called 'The In-Betweens' and one of the members was Alan Johnson, later to become Labour Home Secretary.

In 1966 Arif bought a shop in Tottenham Lane, Hornsey. He was selling greengroceries, particularly catering for the West Indian community, stocking yams, plantains, cassava etc. People would come from Brixton, Hammersmith and all over London, as there were very few shops at that time selling such food. He bought the shop when it had weekly sales of £300. When he later sold the business, it was turning over £1,000 a week.

The shop became a meeting-place where people came to socialise and discuss politics. Arif founded a cooperative with members of the West Indian community in Hornsey where a credit union was already functioning successfully. The shop was also used by the community as a base to leave their weekly contributions for pardner, box-hand or su-su.

Arif was an active member of the Labour Party when living in Hoddesdon and he had also been very active in the trade union movement. He was asked to stand for election as a local councillor, but his interests were developing in a different direction.

A few doors away from the shop stood the office of the *Hornsey Journal* and its editor often came into the shop to buy and discuss. One day Arif said to him: "Why is there always all this negative news about black people in the paper? What about me writing some articles of a more positive nature?" The editor thought it was a good idea, especially as Arif said that he would get some advertising to pay for the page. But the idea was rejected.

happen later, when his house was fire-bombed and he stayed up all night to protect his family.

Arif's active interest in trade unionism, which had begun at the hospital, continued and in 1959 he joined the Labour Party. At London Transport he was also elected as one of the sports organising secretaries for the tennis section. This meant he had more favourable shifts and he was also provided with a telephone, typewriter and other facilities in his home. Arif reflects on this situation: "The people who elected me to this important position were all white and from different garages and jobs. To the best of

Chapter 20

Arif Ali

Publishing the *West Indian Digest*

"From the time you start to live in England it is as if a sea of white faces is always around you. Don't forget this is no small-island. In London alone there are more than eight million people living."
Sam Selvon *Going to Britain?* 1959

"The Anglo-Saxon waxeth great in pride,
And well he may for great have been his gains.
But granting this and what you will beside,
Has he monopoly of wit and brains?"
George C. Rampal, *Georgetown* 1894

"We is people. I, you, you, for we own self. For you and for you and for your own self. We is people with the responsibility for we own self. And as long as we appeal to others, to the authorities, they will do what they want. We have to act for we."
Earl Lovelace *The Dragon Can't Dance* 1979

"I have learnt
from books dear friend
of men dreaming and living
and hungering in a room without a light
who could not die since death was far too poor
who did not sleep to dream, but dreamed to change
* the world"*
Martin Carter (1927-1997) *Looking at your hands*

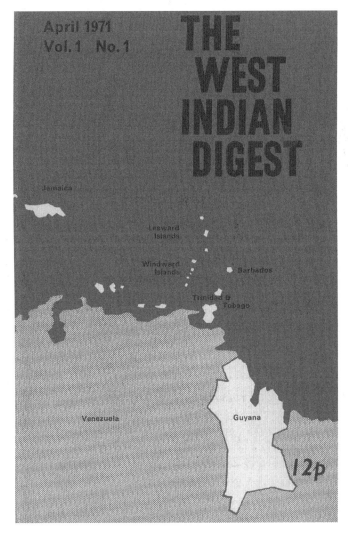

The *West Indian Digest*, April 1971, Vol. 1 No. 1

In 1970 Arif sold the shop to the cooperative which he had founded, much to the annoyance of his father who would not talk to him for weeks! He retained 10% of the business, as his contribution, and agreed to stay with their management for a few months.

Arif cleaning the shop at 137 Tottenham Lane, North London

Members of the co-op SANFA to whom the shop was sold in 1969

With the £5,000 he received, he published his first magazine, the *Westindian Digest*. The first issue appeared in April 1971, size A5 with 50 pages and costing 12p. Its aim was "to improve Community Relations" and in the editorial Arif wrote: "We will endeavour to keep it a simple straightforward magazine so that the ordinary person will find it easy to read."

Arif recalls the importance of this first publication: "That was a very significant moment for me. Apart from its significance to a growing Caribbean community in London, it was a labour of love for me personally. I had served as journalist and editor and had helped with the paste-up, typesetting and the trimming of the magazine. I couldn't stop looking at it even though some of our advertisers didn't think much of the effort."

At this time, most West Indians (71%) regularly read newspapers from the Caribbean, but by the early 1970s they started reading British publications to get news about the Caribbean. According to research by David Pearson, carried out between 1971 and 1973, 17% were now reading papers such as *Westindian Digest* and *West Indian World*.

Besides containing information about the various Caribbean islands and poems by his wife, Pamela, the magazine also tackled the subject of racism. In May 1971 the editorial asked a question that is still relevant today: "Why not write an Afro-West Indian family into Coronation Street?" It also raised an issue which was to pre-occupy teachers and parents throughout the 1970s and beyond: a call to "eradicate racial stereotypes e.g. Ten Little Nigger-Boys, Little Black Sambo, naughty golliwogs".

In July/August Arif recounted an incident in his daughter's school: "A few weeks after my younger daughter started school she came home and told me 'Daddy, my friends call me blackie. I think they were being horrible, but I don't mind.' My daughter was fortunate that her headmistress is understanding and she actually lectured the entire class of five year olds. There was never a recurrence…"

In the same issue the *Westindian Digest* gave a welcome to a new weekly newspaper called the *West*

Ray Luck. international pianist from Guyana, the *West Indian Digest* July/August 1971, Vol. 1 No. 4

The *West Indian Digest*, Nov/Dec 1971, Vol. 1 No. 8

Angela Davis receiving a framed copy of *West Indian Digest* from Ansel Wong

Demonstration against The Immigration Bill, 1971, London

Indian World and wished it "every success". This paper, costing 5p, was founded and edited by Aubrey Baynes who came from St. Vincent. It was later edited by Arif (see next chapter).

The *Digest* was keen to stress its independence: "We get no money from any source other than sales and advertising." It supported a rally for Angela Davis in Birmingham on 15 October, where the speaker was her sister Tania Jordan. And it advertised the "First West Indian Films": *The Right and the Wrong* and *The Caribbean Fox*.

In the October/November issue Arif made a heartfelt plea for more mixing of Indo-West Indians and Afro-West Indians: "When I go to Indo-West Indian functions I meet several white Europeans and when I attend Afro-West Indian functions again, I meet several of the host population, but I seldom see an Afro-Asian mixture."

But the financial situation was getting desperate and Arif had to confront the reality of running such a business. After three issues of the *Digest* he was broke! Advertisers were not paying promptly and the money from sales took two months to come in. After the next three issues he was heavily in debt and could not pay the printers. In six months he had lost £6,000. His gas, electricity and telephone were cut off and his father told him to become a shopkeeper again!

But Arif was determined to go on publishing, despite the difficulties, and it was then that a pivotal meeting took place. The manager of the printing firm told Arif that the owner wanted to see him. With much trepidation he went to his house, to be greeted by a black lady who asked him in to see John Chapman.

Mr Chapman said to Arif: "I like what I'm reading in these magazines, but I don't like you not paying! Talk to me and tell me what it's all about."

Arif replied: "We want to produce something positive about our achievements in this country. I'm not treated as an equal here. I have to work harder than most people to get them to recognise my abilities. I have to be twice as good as every white person I meet. I don't want my colour to be used in a derogatory way."

Mr Chapman listened and then said: "OK, I've heard enough. I'm going to back you." Arif recognises

The *West Indian Digest*, Oct/Nov 1971, Vol. 1 No. 7

Hansib's logo – tribute to John Chapman

The *West Indian Digest*, April 1985, No. 117

the critical importance of this event: "If it wasn't for many white people who have worked with me and are my friends and family, Hansib would not have done so well. This is why the eighth edition of *Third World Impact* was dedicated to John Chapman." His name, represented by the enveloping initial C, was also incorporated into Hansib's logo, along with letters standing for Arif's five children: Kashif, Kamene, Sayrah, Zahid and Shareef.

Westindian Digest went on to be successful as a trailblazing black magazine, supported by the West Indian community who helped with its sale and distribution in shops and at functions. An organiser of one event at Hornsey Town Hall complained that everyone was reading the *Westindian Digest* instead of dancing! After its first year of existence it was selling 5,000 copies a month and by October 1972 was up to 10,000.

Herman Ouseley, who later became the chief executive of the Commission for Racial Equality and then entered the House of Lords, first met Arif around this time. He acknowledges the key role which Arif played: "He has been pivotal in keeping the minority communities in Britain informed about news from a Caribbean/African/developing world perspective, not to be found in the newsprint available. He is the ultimate wheeler-dealer, whose drive is always to get things done."

At this time W. H. Smith, the main newsagent in the country, would not stock a black paper, so Arif decided to do something about it. After phoning the manager's secretary a dozen times with no success, he went to the office himself and was told by the doorman at 10 Fetter Lane that the manager, Mr Triplow, regularly arrived at 9am. The next day Arif was there waiting for him and they entered the lift together. Arif apologised for this manner of meeting and explained his purpose. The outcome was that W. H. Smith agreed for the first time to sell a black UK based monthly publication, and so open the gates for later publications.

In August 1980 Arif brought out a sister paper called *Asian Digest*, priced at 25p. His *Westindian Digest* also continued well into the 1980s when it was edited by Ken Campbell. It was then a glossy A4

production, advertising itself as "a popular home, reception room and campus companion: a monthly selection of quizzical commentaries and human interest statements focussing especially on Caribbean lifestyles, natural history and the liberal arts".

Chapter 21

Arif Ali

West Indian World

"Elaborate strategies were conscientiously devised by the plantocratic bourgeoisie and its state to create the maximum division between Africans and the newly-arrived and cruelly-deceived Asians in the Caribbean. It therefore would have taken a miracle for some of these oppositional attitudes towards Asians not to have been brought among the cultural inventory of Afro-Caribbean people migrating to Britain in the post-war period."
Winston James *Inside Babylon: The Caribbean Diaspora in Britain* 1993

"Westindian Digest magazine under Arif Ali and Robert Govender, Westindian World newspaper under Aubrey Baynes and Arif Ali have always preached a ONE-BLACKNESS line but the word from other black publications has been less clear."
Westindians in Britain 1979

"It became clear that Ali's anti-racist campaigning did not sit well with the printers and some of the staff."
Lionel Morrison *A Century of Black Journalism in Britain 1893-2003*

Aubrey Baynes

In 1971 the *West Indian World* was launched by Aubrey Baynes, with the support of Zeina Mason, Reynold Francis and Conrad Gomes. The first issue came out on 11 June, priced at 5p, and announced itself as "Britain's first national West Indian weekly".

Eighteen months later, however, the paper got into financial difficulties. The situation at the beginning of 1973 had become quite complicated, with Baynes

EDITORIAL

EDITOR: Arif Ali
ASST. EDITORS: Robert Govender, Stephen Bulgin and Premindra Vaniak
ADVERTISING: Carmen Sloan, Lennox Renwick
CIRCULATION MANAGER: John Hughes
NATIONAL DISTRIBUTORS: Continental Publishers and Distributors Ltd.

In Barbados last week Arif Ali, this paper's editor, spoke with passion, feeling and reason on the plight of West Indians in Britain. If ever anyone needed assurance that the **West Indian World** is not a mercenary newspaper concerned only with advertising revenue and profit, but a paper that genuinely cares for the welfare of its people, Arif Ali's straight-from-the-shoulder speech should leave them in no doubt on this score.

As for the authorities in this country the warning is clear: we are not going to allow ourselves to be forcibly repatriated without a fight.

We will not be like the poor Jews of Dachau who went willingly into the gas-chambers believing that they were being assembled to hear an important statement from their oppressors. But we will be like the Jews of the Warsaw Ghetto. Their resistance to Nazi tyranny, their willingness to fight and be destroyed fighting rather than to die on their knees is one of the most glorious episodes in the history of the human race.

We have no desire to engage in any melodramatic rhetoric. The events of the past few months, the burning of black shops, the killing of a black girl in circumstances that suggest political arson, and the ever-increasing brutality of sections of the British police to black people emphasise the need for vigilance on the part not only of black people here, but more importantly, black people in the free states of the Caribbean.

Our brothers and sisters are getting tired of reading about acts of brutality against black people in Britain. They, too, are itching for action.

The fascist thugs of Britain have an insane hatred of blacks: they cannot work out the consequences. But their more literate political masters can. Let them act quickly before the acts of retaliation which many blacks are clamouring for in the Caribbean really start.

Editorial *West Indian World*, 29 June 1973

West Indian World Editor Arif Ali tells of the calamitous consequences of forced repatriation:

BLOOD WILL FLOW

By our Political Correspondent

In one of the most uncompromising speeches made in the Caribbean by a leading Black British leader, Mr. Arif Ali, Editor of the West Indian World and Publisher-Editor of the West Indian Digest, said there would be bloodshed in the streets of Britain if attempts are made to repatriate West Indians against their will.

Arif Ali gives it straight from the shoulder: "I will go down fighting."

Headlines of *West Indian World*, 29 June 1973

suggesting to Arif that the two papers merge and Arif talking about the *Digest* going weekly and then Baynes suggesting that Arif take over the *West Indian World*. Arif feels a bit guilty now, because he played a waiting game and was hesitant to take on the paper's debts as none of the printing bills had ever been paid. He was told that the debts amounted to £8,000, but later discovered they were over £60,000! Also in the office of the *West Indian World* he found piles of unsold papers. They would print 9,000 copies, but only distribute 6,000!

Arif was in a dilemma: "I had mentally considered a weekly publication. On the one hand I had my people looking at a successful business and job security with the *Digest* at our premises in London at Matthias Road. On the other hand I had my thoughts and memories of the criticism we had received over the two years that the *West Indian Digest* had survived. They would say things like: 'Are you still publishing?! Black publications usually only last for a few issues. Black people don't support things like magazines, only dances!' I was aware that no one, until the *Digest* came out in April 1971, had published a regular monthly magazine and no one, until Aubrey Baynes brought out the *West Indian World* in June 1971, had published a regular weekly paper from the black community in the UK."

Arif wanted both papers to survive and to prove the critics wrong: "Between the two publications, we were getting the West Indian community to be aware of the need for togetherness and at the same time informing them of the common difficulties we were all experiencing. I felt that if the *West Indian World* folded, it would reflect poorly on our community and cause ripples for *West Indian Digest* and my future weekly plans. I couldn't sell this sentiment to my team and advisors and decided against their wishes to re-launch the *West Indian World* which had ceased publication mid-April 1973."

On 4 May it was announced in the paper that Aubrey Baynes was suffering from over-work and strain and that Arif Ali would act as Managing Editor. On 25 May it was reported that Aubrey Baynes had tendered his resignation a week previously and that Arif was now the editor. The paper had been saved by Arif securing shares in the company and by other supporters such as the Jamaican property developer Joe Whitter who secured a loan.

Arif set about improving the publicity and distribution of the paper. In June he "toured 13 countries in the Caribbean to appraise Prime Ministers and other statesmen there of the condition of black Britons, their relations with the police, their housing, job and economic problems and the growth of right-wing hostility and violence towards them".

He wanted Caribbean governments to intervene more directly in what was going on in Britain: "Local High Commissions will, in future, be expected to investigate fully such incidents as police brutality towards their subjects and wherever necessary to make strong representations to the authorities concerned. This is an important step and one which will give some comfort to the black Community here which, because of the indifference of most of the Caribbean High Commissions to this issue, has given them the feeling that their servants in these offices whose salaries and allowances are paid for by the tax-payers, are not discharging their duties and responsibilities to their citizens in this country with either efficiency or sincerity."

When he returned, the *West Indian World* (29 June, 1973) appeared with the dramatic headline "BLOOD WILL FLOW". With an echo of Enoch Powell's infamous 'Rivers of Blood' speech in April 1968, Arif stated: "Talking about compulsory repatriation – the streets of London will be flooded with blood before we come out of here."

His editorial was just as hard-hitting: "As for the authorities in this country the warning is clear: we are not going to allow ourselves to be forcibly repatriated without a fight." While not condoning it, he warns of the possibility of "acts of retaliation".

The *West Indian World* prospered at its larger premises, with *West Indian Digest,* in Stoke Newington. The paper campaigned on various educational issues such as the 'bussing' of black children to other schools in London and the "inferior education at the Earl Cowper Middle School" in Chapeltown, Leeds, which had 90% black pupils and a very high turnover of teachers. In November it

ARIF ALI RESIGNS EDITORSHIP

Mr Arif Ali has resigned as Editor of Westindian World and Director of Lenmond Publishing Ltd., publishers of Westindian World.

Mr Ali has taken the decision to resign because of the increasing workload associated with the growth of the paper and his commitment in other fields.

Mr Ali first joined Westindian World on May 4 1973. His resignation has been in effect since November 1st 1976.

Westindian World will continue under the management of the present staff.

How *Westindian World* (12 November 1976) reported Arif's ousting welcomed Darcus Howe as the new editor of the journal *Race Today* and the following month reported that Mary Seacole's grave in Kensal Green Roman Catholic Cemetery had been restored by nurses from Jamaica.

1974 saw Arif flying to Libya (12 July), Cheddi Jagan arrested in Guyana (9 August), and the "first serious radio programme for black people" (29 Nov). The support given by Arif to 'Radio Black Londoners' is acknowledged by its Grenadan presenter Alex Pascall, who realised from the start that they needed to work in tandem. They complemented each other, raising similar topical issues and publicising various black figures who passed through London.

Alex Pascall has known Arif from his days as a shop-keeper and has remained a good friend ever since. He respects Arif, for his business acumen and campaigning spirit: "Arif is a totally Caribbean man, who knows his culture. He remains Guyanese in his speech and has never tried to mimic an Englishman. Wherever Arif is, there is theatre and you cannot miss the actor who is Arif! He tells you the truth in jokes and will tell people what he thinks of them. He is sharp, personable, forthright, cheeky and chatty. Like a village elder, he advises people and he has given opportunities to so many of those who have worked with him.

"Arif has always been in the forefront of the campaign against a racist society. He has annoyed a lot of people and been put under pressure from the British police. His work has brought Caribbean people together, in the tradition of Claudia Jones. He has handed out accolades to members of the Black community, but never wanted one for himself."

In 1975 Arif was speaking at large meetings all around the country, in cities such as Birmingham, Leeds, Northampton and Huddersfield. In Leeds the gathering was attended by 500 West Indians and he was given a standing ovation. In particular they were protesting at the 'Holiday Magic Pyramid Swindle'. An American cosmetics company, along with other companies, had persuaded people to invest £1,500, for example, in goods which they were told would earn them £3,000. Forty finance companies had given easy loans and tens of thousands of people were deceived by the scheme. When Arif called a meeting at his office in Matthias Road, Stoke Newington, "hundreds turned up and packed the place out".

Local committees were set up in fourteen major cities, co-ordinated by James Hunte in Birmingham, to campaign to get people's money back. At its height, there were 36,000 members of the organisation. *West Indian World* was still reporting the campaign in 1977. *Westindians in Britain* recorded that by 1979 over £16m had been recovered. But the cost had been high: "68 suicides and deaths plus 619 people in mental homes are on record as pertaining to the Pyramid Swindle."

Arif's Libyan connection enabled him to sell an extra 1,000 copies of the paper and it was sent to every Libyan Embassy, in 65 countries. This boosted the pen-pals scheme and every day sacks full of mail would arrive at the office from around the world. Arif was also offered £1m, but with strings attached, so he refused. He did, however, accept to publicise Gadhafi's *Green Book*, first published in 1975, over a period of six months, with payment made in advance. Arif agreed with the initial reforms being carried out in Libya, but later disagreed with Gadhafi's way of dealing with opponents.

1976 was a critical year for Arif and the *West Indian World*. At the invitation of the prime minister, Errol Barrow, Arif and his family went to Barbados for a year. This was so that his children could find out about the Caribbean and be educated there for a while. Later, in 1984, he recalled this time: "In 1976 I saw it fit and necessary to take my children home. I would have loved to take them to Guyana, but unfortunately my relationship with the government was a little strained in that period, so I took them to Barbados. My kids spent eleven months in Barbados. They enjoyed it. They went to school there."

The trip to Barbados was also to promote the paper in the West Indies. He managed to persuade leaders such as Burnham (Guyana), Manley (Jamaica) and Gairy (Grenada) to take copies for distribution in their countries and also to advertise in the paper. Barbados took 3,000 copies every week, bringing in thousands of pounds. Caribbean Airlines,

The Times Diary

Bitter battle for black readers

There is a lively and potentially litigious four-sided circulation war brewing among the West Indian newspapers in Britain. Vigorous editorials alleging sellouts and betrayals are being countered with solicitors' letters and threats of writs, while personal insults are being traded with a will among former colleagues who now find themselves on separate sides in the sniping.

The occasion for the outbreak of hostilities has been the launch of a new paper called *West Indian Post*, edited by a South African-born Indian, Robert Govender, and financed by a typesetting firm in south London, Kenafast Ltd. Govender was formerly deputy editor of the oldest established weekly serving the West Indian community in Britain, *West Indian World*, and subsequently editor of a new venture called *Caribbean Post*.

Kenafast, whose directors are two white Londoners, Anthony Bloomfield and Terence Hancock, did typesetting in the past for both *West Indian World* and *Caribbean Post*, and claim to have lost money on both accounts. Their backing for Govender's *West Indian Post* has been denounced as white domination in both the other papers.

To complicate the picture a former editor of *West Indian World*, Arif Ali, says he is shortly to start regular publication of yet another paper, *West Indian Voice*, published in conjunction with a black self-help organization called West Indian Concern. Ali, who claims still to own a controlling interest in *West Indian World*, was none the less dismissed from the editorship of that newspaper in what the workers' co-operative who now run it call a "dramatic coup". Their allegations against him were that he spent too long in the Caribbean and

that he used the paper too much as a vehicle for personal publicity.

Ali says his intention now is to abandon the black chauvinist line he pursued with *West Indian World* and to try to get across "a more positive and integrationist message". He says he does not intend to reply to attacks on him from *West Indian World*, "probably from a little bit of sentiment".

Tony Douglas, the present deputy editor of *West Indian World*, uses unsentimental language when speaking of some of its rivals. "There are a lot of leeches about, trying to make something for themselves out of the sorrow and misery of black people. We intend to say so, right out." West Indians in Britain may be deprived in many respects, but at least they have plenty to read.

The Times records Arif's ousting, 29 March 1977

Some *West Indian World* front covers under Arif's editorship

then owned by Barbados, also agreed to advertise in the paper and in return transport the papers to the Caribbean. As well as all this, Arif travelled back to London for two weeks every month to supervise production.

Things came to a head in the Autumn of 1976 when Arif returned to find that a coup had been organised by the printers and fronted by the staff. The chairman of the printers, Mike Asleep, had wanted Arif to sell him his controlling shares in the paper in order to further his political career. Arif refused, saying that "what he was doing with his publications and what he wanted to achieve would be of benefit to his children and their children in centuries to come".

In an interview with Ionie Benjamin, Tony Douglas, Arif's assistant editor, explained what happened: "We called a meeting in his absence and decided: this can't go on, we've got to get rid of Arif. When he arrived in the office no one wanted to say anything because everyone behaved as if they were frightened of him. We went into what was then his office and I said to him, look, Arif, your time is up, we've had enough. He asked the rest of the staff what they thought and everyone kept quiet. He took the silence to mean a vote of no confidence and he eventually cleared his desk and left."

A few days later, Russell Pierre, Arif's managing editor, asked Arif if he wanted to return, telling him that his desk was still vacant, but he replied, "I'm not prepared to come back." And this was despite the fact that he still owned the paper, with 51% of the shares! His motto was still in operation: "Don't get even, get on." Several of the staff who ousted him came back later to work with him at *Caribbean Times.* During the period of his editorship, from May 1973 to November 1976, Arif and his team established what was often described as "the mouth-piece of the West Indian community and a thorn in the establishment side".

None of what had happened was reported in the paper. The issue of 12 November simply stated: "ARIF ALI RESIGNS EDITORSHIP"! Something of what was going on was reported however in *The Times* Diary (29 March, 1977). Under the sub-heading "Bitter battle

for black readers", it began: "There is a lively and potentially litigious four-sided circulation war brewing among the West Indian newspapers in Britain. Vigorous editorials alleging sell-outs and betrayals are being countered with solicitors' letters and threats of writs. While personal insults are being traded with a will among former colleagues who now find themselves on separate sides in the sniping."

The piece refers to the "launch of a new paper called *West Indian Post*, edited by a South-African-born Indian, Robert Govender" who had earlier been editor of *Caribbean Post*. It also quotes Arif Ali as saying "he is shortly to start regular publication of yet another paper, *West Indian Voice*". It refers to Arif's ousting from West Indian World as a "dramatic coup".

Arif kept the controlling shares in *West Indian World* refusing to sell to Mike Asleep. A year later he passed the shares on equally to members of the coup for next to nothing, creating a co-operative.

The *West Indian World* continued as a co-operative, but ironically Tony Douglas was himself ousted a few years later by Caudley George, after a High Court judgement. By the time it folded in 1985, under the editorship of the Trinidadian Alfred Tang Chow, the paper was becoming increasingly hostile towards Arif. Every other week the Diary entry by John Leigh would insult him, calling him "the Buddha from Guyana", "the self-styled editor of the *Caribbean Times*" and referring to the paper as "his rag".

These attacks culminated in a full-page "world exclusive" by the editor, criticising his "very desirable residence" in Hertfordshire, his business dealings and advertising revenue, his family and friends. The paper was clearly in its death-throws and the following week's issue (30 October, 1985) was its last!

Chapter 22

Arif Ali

Caribbean Times

"The Caribbean Times was in many respects credited with setting the black political agenda and succeeded in doing so because of its editorial integrity, its unique analytical style and its unquestioned status as the political voice of the black community. On the burning issues of the day, it was compulsory reading for progressive British politicians."
Tony Wade *The Adventures of an Economic Migrant* 2007

"Indo-Caribbeans have over the years played an important role in anti-racist politics in Britain, constituting an integral part of what we may call the black movement in this society."
Winston James 1993

"I always said, maybe one day I'll go home, and I did. I never expected anything, but still some of my dreams came true. We have to thank the people at home who stood up to everything, and also the international community for raising their voices."
Miriam Makeba *Homecoming* 2003

After leaving the *West Indian World* Arif concentrated on improving the *Westindian Digest*, changing it from A5 to A4, and continued working on his series of black Who's Who books. He had learnt something from the coup against him: "It educated me and taught me to be more sensitive. I realised the disadvantage of people fearing me and not telling me the truth. If you are more understanding, they are more likely to let you know what they are really

First issue of *Caribbean Times*

What the papers say about *Caribbean Times*

thinking." He decided to start a new paper, which took three years to realise.

In 1981 it materialised - the *Caribbean Times*, a 24-page A3 weekly costing 20p. Arif wanted to launch it on Friday 13 March, despite the misgivings of his staff. This was his birthday and he called it "lucky Friday"!

It was also the second anniversary of the revolution in Grenada that brought to power the New Jewel Movement and its prime minister Maurice Bishop. Arif already had an agreement with Bishop that they would buy 10,000 copies of the paper, so the first issue contained a supplement on Grenada. Support for Grenada was to be a continuing theme in the paper, and when the American invasion took place in 1983, the headline screamed "TRAITORS", branding all those Caribbean governments who supported the actions of the USA. Photographs of their prime ministers covered the front page.

Arif attempting to see Maurice Bishop, imprisoned by Eric Gairy in Grenada 1974

Another of the paper's constant campaigns was support for the Anti-Apartheid struggle in South Africa and calls for the release of Nelson Mandela. This was why the front page in September 1982 expressed such shock at the newly launched paper *The Voice*, whose editor Val McCalla had said that anti-apartheid news was only of "peripheral" interest to black Londoners. McCalla also said that he would not tolerate "his" paper falling under the control of "anti-apartheid conspirators"!

McCalla had come to Britain when he was 15 years old, after being educated at Kingston College, one of Jamaica's top high schools. *The Voice* campaigned particularly on issues related to Black British youth and received an enormous amount of advertising from the Greater London Council and other public bodies. McCalla launched a couple of other magazines, but *The Voice* was his main achievement and it still exists today.

1981 was a momentous year for the black communities in Britain, with the New Cross fire, riots in Bristol, Brixton and Liverpool, and the massive increase in unemployment of young black people. These were regularly reported in the *Caribbean Times*, along with incidents of police brutality and racist attacks. The paper also contained extensive

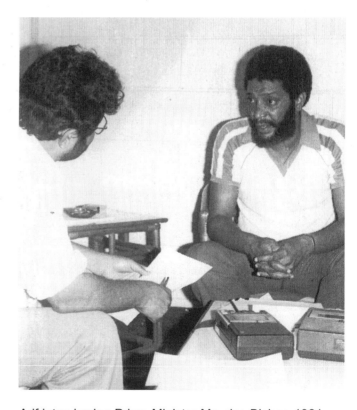

Arif interviewing Prime Minister Maurice Bishop 1981

APOLOGY

WE apologise to our readers for our usual sections of the the paper that were left out this week. We view the Invasion of Grenada with such seriousness that we feel that justice would not have been done had we not given it the coverage that we have.

Next week we return to normal with all our usual sections.

20p

CARIBBEAN TIMES

Weekly — BRITAIN'S BIGGEST — Friday 4th to Thursday 10th November 1983. Issue 139

TRAITORS

AS THE blood of innocent Grenadian women and children stain their country, the real traitors of the Caribbean people sit in their respective countries in the comfort and knowledge that Uncle Ronnie will see them through.

These traitors are Mr. Tom Adams, Prime Minster of Barbados; Mr Edward Seaga, Prime Minister of Jamaica; Miss Eugenia Charles, Prime Minister of Dominica; Mr John Compton, Prime Minister of St. Lucia; Mr Vere Bird, Prime Minister of Antigua and Barbuda, Mr. Milton Cato, Prime Minister of St. Vincent and the Grenadines; Dr. Kennedy Simmonds, Prime Minister of St. Kitts and Nevis; Mr John Osborne, the Prime Minister of Montserrat.

What Price Grenada?

Grenada has been sold out by these states for the pleasure of receiving a few paltry dollars from Washington. These leaders with their 30 pieces of silver should now be made to hang themselves by the criticism of their own people. The clandestine and deceitful manner in which they operate in this crisis have made it impossible for other CARICOM leaders to ever trust them again. The amount of bombs are raining down on the Grenadian people can only be attributed to the collusion of these neo-colonial leaders with their master Ronald Reagan.

Caribbean people who have been fighting for many years to have the sovereignty and independence of these small islands respected by bigger nations are annoyed at the manner in which this whole murderous, nasty, treacherous episode has been conducted.

The Americans are now systemically destroying all the leaders of the New Jewel Movement in Grenada. We have also heard stories of the Americans offering ordinary Grenadians large sums of money if they can identify members of the New Jewel Movement and members of the Peoples Revolutionary Army. This is then followed by

a systematic liquidation of these people.

It has been a testimony to the courage and determination of the Grenadian Army that although they are out numbered six to one, and facing over -whelmingly superior fire power, they have not caved in but have resisted the Americans at every stage. We salute the courage of these brave men and women of Grenada.

These treacherous Caribbean leaders should never be allowed to set foot in London peacefully again. They should be made aware of their despicable action through demonstrations boycotts and whatever methods are at the disposal of the New Jewel Movement in London. Their exports into this country should be boycotted to show them how strong is the feeling against their treacherous actions of meddling and calling in external forces against the people of Grenada in largely something that was an internal matter for the people of Grenada.

These leaders should be given a harsh reception at the Prime Ministers Commonwealth Conference in India later this month.

The Peoples Revolution of Grenada suffered the greatest act of treachery from these reactionary Caribbean leaders who are said to have called in the Americans. This act in itself was a flagrant disregard for the sovereignty of an independent nation. It was a severe breach of international law. There is no moral, political, economic

or social rights that can have allowed these neighbouring countries to be a party to the rape and destruction of the Grenadian countryside.

As the Americans pour men and ammunition into Grenada, as they destroy every vestige independence of the Grenadians these Caribbean leaders should be ashamed of their meddling in the internal affairs of a member country. There can be no justification for the conniving with the most powerful fighting machine to lay waste and destroy Grenada.

Grenada did not present a threat to any of these countries.

Every man, woman and child should be ashamed of the actions of these leaders and their part in the dismantling of the Grenadian revolution.

Their hands are stained with the blood of innocent Grenadians. It is a mockery of America's claim to have gone into Grenada to restore law and order, to save lives.

The harsh realities of the situation is that more people have died as a result of the US invasion than those killed by the Peoples Revolutionary Government or the military take over after Maurice Bishop's death. More buildings have been damaged by the Americans than at any time since the 13th March 1979. In fact more people have been detained by the Americans than at any time since the beginning of the Grenadian Revolution. These facts have been played down by Ronald "cowboy" Reagan and his puppets in the Caribbean.

GRENADA

Tom Adams

P.M. Edward Seaga

P.M. Eugenia Charles

P.M. John Compton

P.M. Milton Cato

P.M. John Osborne

P.M. Vere Bird

P.M. Kennedy Simmonds

Caribbean Times issue 139, 4 November 1983

Leon Mitchell (Jamaican Gleaner), Val McCalla (Voice), Neil Kenlock (Root Magazine), Arif Ali (Hansib), at a meeting to look at the possibility of forming a Black Publishers Association

arts and sports pages and managed to attract a lot of advertising, particularly from Caribbean businesses and London boroughs.

As Tony Wade, a successful businessman from Montserrat, comments: "The moral strength of a community exercised through its newspaper must never be lost on the generation to follow. The paper's influence on change was enormous. Black small businesses benefited from the paper's generous credit-tolerance and sympathetic discounts, thus encouraging entrepreneurship and playing a significant role in the pursuit of wealth creation in the community."

Not everyone, however, was pleased with Arif's hard-hitting political stance. Shreela Flather, for example, who later became the first Asian woman in the House of Lords, first met him in 1980 and says: "I did not get a good reception from the Guyanese 'Mafia', such as Arif and Roy Sawh. In fact some quite nasty things were put in the West Indian papers being published at the time. I did not fit their image of a person who should be involved in race relations. Too middle class and Tory."

They eventually became "really good friends", however, and she pays this tribute: "I think the most

important thing is Arif brought the views of people of Caribbean origin to the forefront. I have some of the books that he published and they are really very informative. I just wish that they had got a wider readership in the mainstream. I have to say that I also enjoyed his company a great deal. He was fun to be with."

After the paper's first year, Arif summed up its position: "Money, inevitably, has been the most formidable of the problems. *Caribbean Times* was launched with a great deal of community backing and goodwill, but its initial financial impact was hardly perceptible. It was not until the riots of last summer that the strong stand taken by the paper on Britain's racial problems finally turned the tide in its favour. But almost immediately afterwards, following adverse publicity in the national Press over its support for certain progressive foreign governments, *CT* suffered a serious loss of advertising revenue for which the increased circulation figures could nowhere near adequately compensate."

He goes on to say: "And yet *Caribbean Times* has proved itself to be a viable concern, answering the need for a strong voice in the ethnic Press. Whilst

Arif, Mendi Msming (ANC representative in the UK and Europe), Lord Pitt, Nelson Mandela (on his first visit to England after release from prison) and Sir Shridath Ramphal

Lord Pitt, Arif and Shridath Ramphal

Earle Robinson (standing third from right)

deliberately catering for the young through its music, sport and fashion coverage, it has never failed to make its weighty contributions on such serious issues as Britain's race relations debate and Third World affairs."

Hansib continued the tradition of community awards, the first of which had been presented to Lord Pitt in 1973. It also supported community activities around the country as Earle Robinson records: "Arif has always supported community initiatives within the Leicester area, for example Leicester Caribbean Carnival, Caribbean Times National Domino Championships, Leicester Caribbean Cricket Club, African Caribbean People in Leicestershire which was a research project organised with the University of Leicester." He characterises Arif as "full of humour and easy to get on with" and concludes: "Arif's contribution as a person and as a publisher has provided a long-lasting resource legacy to the UK, not only to the people from the Caribbean region, but also to the wider UK community."

In January 1983, Arif launched the weekly *Asian Times*, edited by G. D. Govender, to replace the monthly *Asian Digest*, and in April 1984 added the *African Times*, edited by Ken Campbell. He was now publishing 3 weekly papers, 2 monthlies and a magazine called Root, and employing 140 staff! The circulation of *Caribbean Times* peaked at 28,000, but averaged about 13,000. In all the publications, Arif was reaching a readership of about half a million people. With some justification he claims to have changed the thinking of British society. He was also feeding the national press, particularly *The Guardian,* with stories which first appeared in *Caribbean Times*.

Several of the staff who came to work with him stayed for short periods in order to learn their trade. Many have worked for Hansib for more than 15 years. He was the first person to give black people this opportunity to learn first-hand about marketing, distribution, advertising, journalism, editing, design, computing, typesetting and publishing. They could then refer to this apprenticeship when applying for other jobs.

Abiola Awojobi, for example, first met Arif when her Sixth Form organised a visit to Hansib in 1985. She was then able to plan a short work experience placement which was extended during her gap year

The problems and frustrations of an emancipated Muslim girl-Page 3

20p ASIAN TIMES

Warning to Kidnap fathers Page 5

The Triumph of Gandhi Pages 12-13

Friday 28th January 1983　A Campaigning Weekly　Issue No. 1

Controversy over top law job

CRE CHIEF BACKS COLOUR BAR

KUTTON MENON, the Senior Legal Officer of the Commission for Racial Equality, who has been in the forefront of the fight against racial discrimination over the last five years is taking the CRE to court. He is alleging that the CRE practised racial discrimination against him when they refused him promotion to the newly created post of Legal Director (salary £19,612 per annum), which was given to John Whitmore, a white barrister with no experience of race relations law.

Kuttan Menon holds an LLM degree from Leicester University and won all the major employment test cases under the 1976 Race Relations Act.

John Whitmore got a first in Law at Oxford and lectured for seven years. He has not fought any race cases in his five years as a barrister in Leicester.

Kuttan Menon is of Indian origin while John Whitmore is a white Englishman.

The Legal Director's salary is £19,612.

To substantiate his case, Kuttan Menon asked for information about the qualifications and experience of other candidates for the job but Peter Newsam, the new Chairman of the CRE and former Chief Education Officer of ILEA, refused him this information on the ground of confidentiality saying he had to consult the other candidates first to see if they had any objections.

It is ironic that the head of the CRE should use the argument of confidentiality to deny Menon access to vital evidence. Newsam is obviously familiar with a well known test case at the House of Lords in which Menon argued, with the full support of the CRE, that applicants in a race-discrimination case would find it impossible to establish the fact of discrimination without access to what Menon

Menon - a masterly advocate

called "vital comparative evidence about other candidates."

We tried to contact a number of CRE personnel for their views on the Menon affair, but obviously intimidated by Newsam's well known aversion to any contacts with the black media, they refused to talk. However, one very responsible voice has spoken in Menon's favour. Geoffrey Bindman, a solicitor with 20 years experience of race relations legislation in Britain and America, and formerly legal adviser to the Race Relations Board and the Commission for Racial Equality, told the *London Times* last week: "Kuttan Menon has been a very able advocate for those who would appear to be a clear case of racial discrimination in the Menon affair.

industrial tribunals. Most of the successful cases are the result of his efforts."

Our Political Editor writes: Those who hoped that Peter Newsam, with his Barbados background and his reputation as a thinker, would prove to be more tactful than the clumsy and maladroit David Lane, whose weak and ineffective chairmanship was tainted with anti-black bias, have been given a reminder in the Menon affair that Lane's successor, too, is almost in the same mould.

The tragic-comic image of the CRE is still as strong as ever, and it seems that both racists and anti-racists will be united in their derision of the paradox of an organisation set up to weaken discrimination actually practising such discrimination itself. There are many well-documented cases where the possession of a white skin has overshadowed merit in job selection and promotion within the CRE.

What is astonishing about Newsam is his rather rash bull-in-the-China shop tactic. Given the uncomfortable time his predecessor had, one would have expected him to test the waters before he committed himself to an emasculated Code of Practice, and backed with such enthusiasm what would appear to be a clear case of racial discrimination in the Menon affair.

The black community will not take kindly to the shabby treatment of Kuttan Menon, a masterly, conscientious and very successful advocate for equality of opportunity.

It is precisely because of such hypocrisy that the CRE has such a lowly standing among the ethnic minorities.

The next time someone complains of racial discrimination they will be wary of insisting that they have access to comparative records for fear that they will have thrown back at them the principle now dictatorially established by Newsam that such access would be a breach of confidentiality. In a single, ham-handed decision Newsam has thus undermined a vital principle in the struggle against racial discrimination. Now we can expect every racist employer in the land to cite the chairman of the CRE as the authority for the so-called confidentiality principle.

OUR NEXT ISSUE

Please note that our next issue appears on February 11 and weekly thereafter.

WHERE WE STAND

THE FIRST thing to remember about the *Asian Times* is that it is a campaigning newspaper. It is not being published for profit nor will it be a tame spokesman for a very tame conservative Asian establishment.

While we welcome Asian enterprise and success in small business where many have wrought miracles in a declining retail trade and have saved many high-streets from the stench of inner city decay, it will be highly misleading to suggest that Asians in trade comprise the majority of the population.

Indeed available statistics suggest that they are a small minority and

FIRST WE HAD E.T. – THEN S.T. – NOW WE'VE GOT A.T.

ASIAN TIMES

that the bulk of Asians make up the labour force of this country. One of the dangers of exaggerating Asian commercial success is, first it tends to give the impression that all Asians are prosperous and doing well, and secondly it reinforces racist envy which already manifests itself in attacks and vandalism on Asian shops and property.

Like the Jews of pre-war Germany in their newsagents, tailor shops, bakeries and small textile factories similar to Bangladeshi establishments in the East End of London, the Asians are a very visible minority. While the Jew-haters among the Nazis waited until there was a complete breakdown of law and order before they raced down the streets smashing up Jewish shops and kicking and beating up their owners with the encouragement of the police and civil authority, British right-wing thugs, in a supposedly well-policed society, daily fling bricks through Asian shop windows with impunity.

This is a regular occurrence throughout the country and the viciousness of these thugs is matched by the smug indifference of the police in London, Bradford, Birmingham, Leeds etc. The fact that very few of the Asian-haters are caught and punished would suggest that there is strong sympathy with such thuggery in the Met and other police forces.

The Asian worker quietly going about his business, is not safe either. Not a week goes by without attacks on Asian persons or their homes, with crazed arsonists resorting to deadly petrol-soaked objects which are pushed through doors when the occupants are asleep.

Hundreds of Asians have been badly beaten up, many have been murdered and several families wiped out in arson attacks.

There is naturally a temptation among the more prosperous Asian trading class to distance itself from the Asian working class, to feel that they are safe and secure in the middle class areas they are moving into, but the attacks on their shops should be a warning that such a segregationist attitude is short-sighted.

We have no sympathy with any section of the Asian community, be it Indian, Pakistani, Chinese or Malaysian which believes that a policy of cowardice, compromise and meekness can bolster its own position. Such an attitude can only play into the hands of those who seek to divide and weaken us.

Ultimately we are in the same boat. If today racist thugs can smash up Asian council homes, nothing will prevent them tomorrow from launching similar attacks on individual Asians in middle class areas. However clumsy right-wing thugs may be, their intelligence sources seem to be extremely good and they will have no difficulty in identifying

Continued on P. 4

Asian Times first issue, 28 January 1983

Watch out for our next issue - April 27th - and weekly thereafter!

No. 1   Lucky Friday 13th April 1984.   A Campaigning Weekly   20p   "AFRICA MUST UNITE"

APARTHEID RACE — Zola Budd leads

The granting by the Home Office of a citizenship status to Zola Budd, the South African woman 5,000 metre runner, has led to a flood of applications to the British embassy in South Africa, for British citizenship.

The Home Secretary Leon Brittan granted Zola Budd citizenship on Friday 6 April. Since then, the British diplomatic missions in South Africa have been swamped with South African sports men and women, who are barred from international competition because of the apartheid policies of their country. Hundreds of other citizens are also in the queue - all seeking British citizenship.

Miss Budd 17, applied for a British citizenship on the grounds that her grandfather was born in Britain. The subsequent approval of her application by the Home Secretary raised questions from the Labour Party and other organisations as to why her case was given priority.

Home Office Minister David Waddington admitted that Zola had been given exceptional treatment. He said that it would have been "awful" if she had not been given the opportunity of applying for the Olympic games due in Los Angeles this year.

The African National Congress (ANC) director of information in London, Mr. Francis Meli said the Home Office decision was saddening. He said: "I feel there are political motivations behind the granting of the citizenship. If Zola was black we would be hearing a different story. If people think granting Zola a citizenship is a human rights case, they should think about apartheid policies in South Africa. I feel she has been let in through the back door."

A spokesman for the Anti Apartheid Movement said the Home Office had acted hastily in granting Zola a citizenship. He said: "One can only

comment that the Home Office allowed Zola through the back door. From what we have heard about her comments, she is not even against apartheid in South Africa. She was reported as having said that apartheid was there before her and it will still be there after she is dead."

Miss Fiona Mactaggart, general secretary of the Joint Council for the Welfare of Immigrants said she was angered by the favour shown by the Home Secretary, to Zola's application. She said Zola had been given priority over thousands of other people whose cases were more deserving.

Clear contradiction

South Africa has ruled that Zola would be able to retain her apartheid citizenship. This contradicts the country's law which requires that South African passport holders do not hold dual citizenship. Zola has apparently been made an exception to the rule. The authorities are clearly motivated by her prospects in competing with international runners and offering an opportunity to promote the country's image as an equal among the world's best athlete.

Now that Zola's application has sparked other applications from people claiming British citizenship, and wishing to further their sporting careers amongst the world's top competitors, the issue is likely to embarass the Home Office.

South Africa has about 40 per cent of its white population of 5 million known as English speakers. It is believed that many of them can make the same descendency claim as Zola.

Meanwhile, the secretary of the Anti-

Apartheid Movement, Mike Terry, has said that his organisation's officials will be meeting the producer of Channel 4 News following the showing on television of a South African propaganda film programme. "Target Terrorism, considered by the AAM to be libelous, was made for South African television and its seven minute edited version was shown on Channel 4 News recently. This took place a day after the South African authorities had blamed the ANC for a car blast in Durban which killed three people.

Mr Stewart Purvis, Channel 4 News producer, refused to comment to African Times saying: "In the light of the Anti-Apartheid movement anticipating taking legal action, I am not prepared to comment."

The AAM believes that "Target Terrorism" is part of the South African government's campaign to get Margaret Thatcher to close down the offices of the ANC in London.

Refugees take on aid agencies.

By Wiseman Khuzwayo

INTERNATIONAL aid agencies have come under fire from refugees in Africa for the way they administer schemes without consultation with the refugees they are meant to be helping.

A recent conference in Oxford attended by 150 people, comprising African refugees, government officials, aid agency staff and academics heard criticisms levelled against the United Nations High Commission for Refugees (UNCHR) for the way it has handled its programmes.

Most of the refugees participating had been flown in directly from the camps in Africa. The UNHCR officials at the conference almost gave credence to the accusations against them; whilst everyone else lived and

dined at a hall of residence, the agency officials lodged themselves in a five star hotel!

Some of the participants gave a report of the conference at the Africa Centre, in London, last week. They praised the organisers of the conference for having given refugees a chance to take part in deliberations about their lives and their future.

Ahmed Karadawi, Assistant Commissioner for Refugees in the Sudan and one of the organisers of the conference, said there was a lot of inconsistencies in the treatment of refugees and talk about them had involved much mystification.

"Refugee programmes involve external aid, but throughout the years, instead of helping

Continued on P.20

Kinnock pledges support for ANC

"The Labour Party is in solidarity with the South African liberation movement", said Mr. Neil Kinnock, in his welcome to Oliver Tambo, President of the ANC. Mr. Kinnock also pledged his support for the ANC. When African Times asked Mr. Kinnock at a recent meeting, how he hoped to put his pledge into practice, with regards to economic and military disinvestment in South Africa, he said: "We will give financial and material assistance to the liberation movements of South Africa ... actively supporting the imposition of UN military and economic sanctions. (See page 20)

African Times first issue, 13 April 1984

Abiola Awojobi

before attending Birmingham University, as she recalls: "I'll never forget how, after I was coming up to the end of my year's work experience at Hansib, Arif cleverly tried to entice me into staying on to work with the company. This would have meant losing my university place for the time being, which I didn't want to do. So we came to a happy compromise. I went to university and Hansib offered me a job during all my vacations.

"It suited us both perfectly and I was able to blend my studies with enhancing my media and writing skills, as well as of course earning some money.

"During this time I learned about research, writing techniques, interviewing people – a wealth of skills which over the years I have used and built on again and again, from my first job on the BBC Radio West Midlands 'Calabash' programme, which I produced for four years, to being producer on the flagship Radio Four programme 'Woman's Hour' and my current job as a producer on CBeebies Radio.

"One of the highlights of my career at Hansib was interviewing the author Maya Angelou when I was eighteen years old. She was incredible and I was chuffed when she remembered me over ten years later when I met her again whilst working on 'Woman's Hour'. The words she spoke to me all those years ago at Hansib still ring in my ears – 'Easy reading is damned hard writing.' It's a motto that has motivated and inspired me throughout my media career and I thank Arif for giving me the opportunity to hear those words."

This aspect of Arif's work is confirmed by Juliet Alexander, Guyanese co-presenter of Black Londoners on BBC Radio London: "I first met Arif when he was editor of the *Caribbean Times*. I loved his energy. He always seemed to have a project on the go and was very enthusiastic about everything. He is without doubt a pioneer in the field of publishing in the UK. He kept us 'immigrants' connected with news from back home. He also, very importantly, offered training and work experience to countless aspiring journalists (at a time when racism and prejudice limited their career choices). Many proficient journalists who now work in a variety of media owe their first early break to Arif Ali and his publications."

Another Guyanese, Christopher Johnson, came from Guyana to work for Arif at Hansib in 1993. He later went on to complete his doctorate and establish himself as a business management consultant. He says: "Mr. Ali's contribution to publishing in Britain is colossal" and he recalls working with him at the *Caribbean Times*: "I remember in the early 1990s his campaigning style towards some public officials who showed no interest or real consideration for issues such as structural poverty, economic deprivation and social exclusion. Mr. Ali often convinced officials that it was in their 'best interest' to help resolve intractable problems rather that to 'fester them'. On the occasion of the Stephen Lawrence and Joy Gardner deaths, his company,

Maya Angelou with Arif

Hansib Publications, took a provocative stance by staging persistent campaigns that eventually affected significant changes in the Establishment."

In 2009 Christopher Johnson wrote a book entitled *British Caribbean Enterprises: A Century of Challenges and Successes* and refers to Arif: "Such was Ali's potency and consistency for over a generation, until the late 1990s, that the name Hansib became synonymous with (campaigning for) universal minority rights, social justice and black economic liberation."

From the start, Arif was involved in black political organisations, such as the Indian Workers Association. He was also Public Relations Officer for the West Indian Standing Conference, an umbrella organisation of over forty African and Caribbean groups in the UK. From 1997 to 2002 he was a member of the Caribbean Advisory Group set up by the British Government to give advice on Caribbean affairs in the UK and the Caribbean. In 1997, the European Year Against Racism, he received the Gold Standard Individual Winner award.

Jenni Francis, a public relations executive, has known Arif for thirty years. She acknowledges his political influence and historical legacy: "Arif must

take credit for many political careers in the UK and across the Caribbean. He is a very special individual with tremendous vision, unstoppable energy and a serious commitment to providing a legacy and resource for Britain's African, Asian and Caribbean communities. Arif has touched many people's lives. He is loyal and supportive. I have always respected his incisive mind and unbridled tongue, plus that infectious sense of humour."

Sharon Atkin, former Lambeth councillor and chair of the Labour Party Black Sections, confirms this view: 'Arif is a very kind person who puts the needs of visible minorities ahead of personal gain or aggrandisement. The newspapers and magazines were at the cutting edge of politics, arts, sports, international affairs, fashion and community interests. The opportunities for young and older people to gain both experience and invaluable training in an organisation that produced both quality books and magazines, and also the Hansib Awards, gave many the start they needed to move on to prestigious employment in broadcasting, print journalism and publishing.'

In 1984 Arif recorded his publishing manifesto: "When people are dying in prison and on the streets

of Britain, when they can't get jobs and their children are being pushed into homes and subnormal education and life is at stake, then I have a feeling, and that's my opinion, that blacks in Britain are on a war footing, and that's when I make that decision. 'Do I publish this article which can only be damaging to the black community?' And when you consider that you have press that are so racist that they only report on black people in the light of crooks and robbers and no-gooders, and when they wilfully don't publish things of achievement, then again I reconsider and say, 'I am, I must be, on a war footing.'"

One of his greatest achievements was to persuade local authorities to advertise jobs in the paper, after lobbying them face to face. Then when he realised that they were advertising for cooks, porters and doormen, he argued that they should also be advertising for architects, accountants and personal assistants! His success can be seen in copies of the paper, with sometimes ten or a dozen whole pages devoted to local authority posts of all kinds.

On a recent trip to Guyana, in an interview for the *Starbroek News*, Arif outlined the invaluable role the *Caribbean Times* played in defining the relationship between the Caribbean and the United Kingdom: "Apart from its role as a voice for Caribbean people in Britain, the *Caribbean Times* also helped West Indians to understand what was taking on back home. The newspaper also played a role in helping policy makers in London to better understand the Caribbean. Additionally, United Kingdom-based businesses with Caribbean interests came to regard the *Caribbean Times* as an indispensable advertising medium."

"When people are dying in prison and on the streets of Britain, when they can't get jobs and their children are being pushed into homes and subnormal education and life is at stake, then I have a feeling, and that's my opinion, that blacks in Britain are on a war footing, and that's when I make that decision. 'Do I publish this article which can only be damaging to the black community?' And when you consider that you have press that are so racist that they only report on black people in the light of crooks and robbers and no-gooders, and when they wilfully don't publish things of achievement, then again I reconsider and say, 'I am, I must be, on a war footing.'"

Chapter 23

Arif Ali

Book Publishing

"Books, magazines and newspapers have provided the vehicle where writing 'black' is expressed in various forms. This is where a written expression of experiences and theorising about the concerns and issues within black communities takes place." Mekada Graham 2005

"In the past great achievements and devoted community leaders and workers died without recognition, without their work being documented. That does not happen any more and the current edition of Westindians in Britain *is yet another testimony of some first rate scholarship by the editor of* Westindian Digest.*"* Robert Govender 1979

Hansib Publications, founded in 1970, was named after Arif's parents, Haniff and Nazibun (Sibby), and in 1973 the first book was published. This was a Who's Who, entitled *Westindians in Great Britain*, and the following year the second edition came out. Arif explained that its purpose was "to inspire further those members of our community who are in leading positions of responsibility".

Amongst its 300 snapshots were those of McDonald Bailey, the hundred metres record holder; another Trinidadian Trevor McDonald; Carmen Sloan, from St Kitts, who was advertising manager of the *West Indian World*; Cy Grant, the Guyanese actor and singer; Trinidadian novelist Sam Selvon; and the Jamaican singer I Roy. Arif sums up the aim of the book: "It helps also to reinforce our belief in ourselves that we can – in spite of the difficulties confronting us – be creative and achieve."

McDONALD Trevor

Born Trinidad 16 August, 1939. Married with two children. Arrived for the second time in U.K. in 1969. Worked with B.B.C. World Service; joined Independent Television News in January, 1973. Writes for several news agencies, newspapers and magazines. Undoubtedly one of their best reporters. Lives in Guildford, Surrey. Plays cricket and lawn tennis. Thinks "It is unfortunate that Black people should consistenly be regarded as a problem."

SLOAN Carmen

Advertisement Manageress Westindian World,
Born Basseterre, St. Kitts. Arrived U.K. December 1965. Enjoys reading, dancing, discussions, tennis and meeting people.

GRANT Cy

Guyanese actor and singer. Member of G.L.A.A. Drama panel. Qualified barrister. Married with three children. Now writing about Black experience.

SELVON Samuel

Writer.
Lives in South East London.
Born San Fernando, Trinidad. Arrived U.K. 24 years ago. Self Educated. Wrote ten novels which include "A Brighter Sun" the classic "The Lonely Londoners" (recently reissued) by Longman Caribbean. Paperback 65p, Cased £1.50 and the "Plains of Caroni." Enjoys reading and tennis.

Pen Portraits

It was launched at the Hilton Hotel in London and Arif ensured its sales by asking each person in it to buy 5 copies for friends and relatives. The flip-side of its success was that it revealed certain individuals to the tax collectors! One of those included in the book, the Jamaican Dudley Dryden, ironically called it a "book of crooks"!

But as Arif says, it certainly showed people that there were Caribbean achievers in Britain: "Previously our West Indian community had nothing going for them. Every newspaper you picked up, from the nationals to the locals, had pages of us as muggers, criminals, wife-beaters etc. I said to myself, I'm mixing with this community all the time and we're not that way. That's something I must correct."

By the fourth edition, in 1979, *Westindians in Britain* had grown to A4 size and contained over 200 pages. It is dedicated to Sonny Ramphal from Guyana, who became Secretary-General of the Commonwealth in June 1975. In the Foreword, Robert Govender calls the book "a treasure-house of vital information providing background that is indispensable to historical study": "As a community we are woefully short of written records, hence the fact that we have to rely on an oral tradition to recreate some of the grander moments of our turbulent history."

By the fifth edition in 1982, it had changed its name to *Third World Impact*. The sixth edition was dedicated "To the Young Black People of Great Britain" and the seventh to Nelson Mandela. The last edition in 1988 had grown to 512 pages, dedicated to John Chapman, "without whose support it would have probably been impossible to sustain our work, particularly in the early days". It contained a photo of the four recently elected black MPs. One of them, Keith Vaz, says: "I have always regarded Arif Ali as a most astonishing person with a wonderful character, generous in heart and spirit. He has supported so many noble causes on behalf of the ethnic communities."

In the 1980s Arif started publishing other books and some of the key titles he recalls are *50 Great West Indian Test Cricketers*, *Rasta and Resistance* and *The Great Marcus Garvey*. Again, the reason for publishing was the lack of black books in Britain. Arif

I Roy

Arif with Paul Boateng, Keith Vaz, Bernie Grant and Diane Abbott

Arif with Jesse Jackson (third from left), Diane Abbott and Bernie Grant

Arif presenting Muhammad Ali, the guest of honour at a Hansib Gala event 1982, with a copy of *Westindians in Britain*

also noticed the absence of books about Indian Caribbeans and so produced titles such as *India in the Caribbean*, *The Other Middle Passage*, *A New System of Slavery*, *Coolie Odyssey* and books about Cheddi Jagan, Rudy Narayan and Shridath Ramphal. Hansib titles have also been translated into many languages, including Arabic, Hindu, Urdu, Swahili, French, German, Italian, Spanish and Mandarin.

In 1988 Arif edited a book about Antigua and Barbuda and this was to be the start of a series about Caribbean countries, including Dominica, Grenada, Barbados, Saint Lucia, Trinidad and Tobago and Anguilla, culminating in Guyana in 2006 and Jamaica

in 2010. Many of the books have gone into several editions and have clearly helped these countries to develop their tourist industries and publicise their investment opportunities.

In 1997 Arif finally sold his newspaper titles in order to concentrate on book publication, which he considers to be less ephemeral. Hansib is still the biggest and most diverse black book publisher in Britain and Arif's aim for the near future is to double his number of publications to over 400.

Chapter 24

Arif Ali

Going Home

"So doan tell me 'bout Guyana.
Ah jus doan want to hear.
Doan tell me how t'ings deh so bad now,
every man Jack livin' in fear;
how dey usin' dey head
jus' to ketch a li'l bread
and how 'class' like it jus' disappear.
I am a son of Guyana, de lan' dat I love so dear,
Ah swear – to me Gaad! – ah gine back deh,
but, chief, ah cyan' mek it dis year.
Michael Gilkes *Son of Guyana*

"If you go ah new place, na cuss where you ah come from."
Guyanese Proverb

When Arif came to Britain in 1957, like most West Indians at the time, his aim was to return after five or six years. In fact he wanted to enter Guyanese politics. He had come to study law or economics, but found the formal system of education too restricting. His immediate task was to earn money so he could send some back home. He also got married early on and soon had a family of five children to support. At this time he says: "Guyana was in my mind all the time."

Ten years after his arrival, however, while running his shop in Hornsey, he made a decision to stay here and records, "I broke off with Guyana mentally." He felt he must concentrate on his family. It was a troubled time in Guyana, with race riots and the authoritarian government of Burnham. In his papers Arif had been critical of this government and also when Jagan took over, so was wary about his reception, as he had been threatened: "Why should I go back to Guyana and possibly get killed like Walter Rodney."

He also realised that here in Britain he actually had a bigger audience and readership of West Indians whom he could influence than back home in Guyana. So he stayed away for several decades. Eventually he returned to plan a book on Guyana and, when this was published in 2006, he was praised by President Bharrat Jagdeo at the book launch: "Arif, I am very pleased that you could just come up here and talk about the shape of your feet. Normally, people would not do that. [In his speech Arif had referred to the fact that he had wide feet because he did not wear shoes until he was in his teens!] But sometimes we are even ashamed of our accent; we want to adopt other people's accents because, somehow, we think it makes us better people, and more modern, and we would be more accepted. From that perspective, I am glad that you mentioned your feet. We are a unique people. We are different from other peoples. We have our weaknesses but we have our strengths, too, and we should all be proud of our upbringing and our past. I am very proud of you, too, because you are Guyanese and you have been serving another country, and the world. Arif, your name will go down in history as helping to change the perception of this country."

Two years later, when Carifesta was held in Guyana, Arif again went back, launched sixteen books in Georgetown, mounted a permanent display at the National Park and sold six million dollars worth of books for two million dollars. Arif called it "an

Front cover of *Guyana* Book

investment in reading". He gave several Hansib publications to the National Library and donated several books to serve as prizes for competitions being arranged by the Ministry for Education.

Arif noticed "what appears to be the loss of the reading habit among younger Guyanese" and wanted to address the problem: "That is why I am so concerned that Guyana move to a position where writers can have access to the best publishing facilities and where people, children in schools and people who read generally, can access good, well-presented books at affordable prices. If we can create a strong publishing industry we can restore the culture of reading in Guyana."

He also made an attack on the practice of copyright infringement in Guyana whereby published texts were copied and sold at cheaper prices. He understood "the affordability issue", and offered a solution: "If Hansib is able to secure a market for quantities of its own books comparable to the amounts being copied, we will be able to provide those books at more affordable prices."

So Arif had come full circle. He had completed a long journey: from bare-foot Guyanese country boy to great metropolitan publisher, and back to Guyana. He is the first to admit that he had the help of African, Asian and Caribbean communities up and down Britain, of hundreds of people who worked with him and thousands who bought his publications. Above all, he had the support of his family. It was truly a communal effort, reflecting his early enthusiasm for the co-operative movement.

Chapter 25

Arif Ali

Conclusion

"Arif is a humble man. I don't know if he has received any major awards for his work as a publisher. He certainly deserves one. I have always held him in the highest esteem. Every time I ask him how he keeps looking so young and healthy, he says: 'Mangoes, Shango, Mangoes!' What a lovely man!"
Shango Baku 2009

"Everybody rights, not only Indian."
Tiger, in Sam Selvon's *A Brighter Sun* 1952

"Arif is noted for his irreverence and acerbic wit, not being fazed by authority or notoriety and this enables him to engage with any individual or scenario, no matter how tense, sensitive or controversial. He remains an unsung hero and in many respects this was a consequence of his deliberate efforts to be the king-maker rather than occupy any regal position."
Ansel Wong 2009

Despite all his success, Arif has remained with his feet on the ground. It is not surprising that he would not accept a knighthood or a peerage. Navnit Dholakia, formerly of the Commission for Racial Equality and now Deputy Leader of the Liberal Democrats in the House of Lords, comments on Arif's informal style and common touch: "Arif never dressed up in formal suits or ties whatever the event. His trademark was the simplicity he displayed. We shared many a dinner at his publishing house. It was always Roti and Dhal from the West Indian take-away."

Jan and Joy Carew at Arif's home in Hertfordshire

Navnit Dholakia (second left) and Mrs Dholakia at Hansib's Community Awards, 1987

Arif with four of his Managing Editors: Ken Campbell (West Indian Digest), Russell Pierre (West Indian World and Caribbean Times), Prakash Singh (Asian Times) and Stephen Bulgin (African Times).

From Left to Right: Jan Carew, Arif Ali, Ivan Van Sertima, and Edward Scobie, New York, 1990. *Photo:* Jacqueline L. Patten-Van Sertima.

Similarly Ros Howells, who also entered the House of Lords, comments: "Arif was always at the back while he pushed others forward – those he trained, those he encouraged and those he recognised."

This aspect of Arif's character is confirmed by Simon Woolley, who organised Operation Black Vote: "With a man of so much power and clout, he never gave the appearance that he was better than you. On the contrary, he is a most accessible man. He acutely understood the need for African, Caribbean and Asian unity. He embodied that spirit."

The famous Guyanese novelist, Jan Carew, who was also a predecessor as a Caribbean publisher and journalist in Britain, sums Arif up: "I was a guest at his house on several occasions and my first impression of him was that he was bold and fearless. His considerable gifts as a public figure are by no means fully recognized. He has been able to make a success of the multiple enterprises that he has undertaken in his lifetime and he has done this with compassion and a generosity of spirit."

Arif's roots are in Guyana. It is clear how much Guyanese history and culture have influenced him and, although now a British resident, he still sees himself as a West Indian. He is part of a long history of Caribbean publishing in Britain, a tradition which he has so ably enhanced and will continue to do so.

The Publication of *Guyana*

The book *Guyana* was launched by President Bharrat Jagdeo on the 8th July 2006 at a gala reception at the Meridian Pegasus Hotel, Georgetown. Over 400 guests attended the launch, which was broadcast live on TV and radio nationwide. The Master of Ceremony for the event was Ron Robinson. The other speakers were Arif Ali, Chief Executive of Hansib Publications and editor of the book 'Guyana' and Capt. Gerry Gouveia. The West Ruimveldt boys choir sang the song, Born in the Land of the Mighty Roraima. The Guyana Police Band and Tassa Drummers provided the entertainment. The event was organised from the President's office by Jennifer Webster, Permanent Secretary Office of the President; Vic Persaud, Head of Protocol; Lt. Col. Francis Abrahams, ADC to the President and Arif Ali with support of several other people.

Excerpt from Ron Robinson's opening remarks:
"I think when you see this book, 'Guyana', you will say that certainly this will enhance any drive that we have with regard to tourism and it certainly will be placing Guyana around the world as a conversation piece, as a place that will be visited more and more. It is beautifully done. But let me not tell you about it, the Chief Executive of Hansib Publications and Editor of *Guyana*, is of course, Arif Ali, and it is his brainchild. It was born out of his concept. Please welcome Arif Ali to tell you about *Guyana*."

Edited version of Capt. Gerry Gouveia speech who spoke after Arif Ali's presentation:
"Arif, I want to tell you about the partnership between the public and the private sector. We don't see this book as a Government book, not at all. In fact we see it as a Guyana book. We see it as a book that was done jointly with the Government and the private sector. A partnership that we don't take very lightly but one that is taken very, very seriously. When Arif spoke to me about this publication a few months ago I was personally very, very excited and immediately pledged my support both in my personal capacity as Chairman of the Roraima Group of Companies and also as the President of the Georgetown Chamber of Commerce. I was excited because all during my time when I served for the five terms as President of the Tourism and Hospitality Association of Guyana and even now as I serve as a Vice Chairman of the Guyana Tourism Authority I always looked with envy at the other countries that had such a treasure. A pictorial and detailed, high quality souvenir publication and I always wanted to strangle you Arif and say why don't you come and do one for Guyana. But I knew with all my heart one day that one day Guyana would look wonderful in a book like this and today we have it. Thank you very, very much.

"The diaspora, those of you who have been following the news, will see that we have been working very hard to tap into the resources of our Guyanese living overseas. We feel very strongly that some of Guyana's greatest assets are the members of our diaspora and you have demonstrated that in no uncertain terms. Thank you very, very much for doing this wonderful work for Guyana.

"This publication provides an opportunity for the world beyond Guyana to see us in a positive light and only God knows we need to project that positive light. So we have a real challenge and this book will help us tremendously in positioning ourselves as the only English-speaking country in the continent of South America and people will start to know that now. We have really suffered too long because of our relatively unknown status in the world. Today, this publication serves to fill that information void. But more importantly, not only will this book bring visitors to our shores, it will bring investors and this country is open for investment. The investment criteria are there. The fiscal incentives are there for the private sector to grow. What we need is to get the word out there and this book will certainly help to let the world know that Guyana is open to invest and ready for tourism. Ready to offer a tourism product that is unequalled.

"It is my hope Mr President that this book will find itself in every hotel lobby, every library, the reception area of every office in both the public and the private sector, every reading room and in every bookstore. I would also expect that the Government of Guyana would furnish our diplomatic missions overseas as well as international organisations with copies of this remarkable publication. I would also like to urge Guyanese to use this book as a gift item to families overseas, send it to your friends as a souvenir of Guyana. I would urge you to seriously give consideration to the reprinting of this book since I have every reason to believe that it would be very popular with visitors to Guyana.

"Once again, I would like to thank you for this wonderful publication on behalf of the private sector and the country in general. Thank you very much."

Ron Robinson:

"Certainly I think we all in Guyana can proudly say that we have a President who has always supported moves such as this; a President who has thrown his weight behind any effort to promote our country in a positive way. When you look at this book you will see that he will proudly endorse 'Guyana' the publication. I now have the honour of inviting our President Bharrat Jagdeo to address us".

President Bharrat Jagdeo:

Thank you. Colleagues of the Cabinet - those who are here – Arif, members of the Diplomatic Corps, Ladies and Gentlemen. First of all let me say that I am extremely pleased to be here and for Arif's sake I just think I need to give an explanation. (Arif Ali, during his presentation earlier had remarked on the few empty seats reserved for Ministers). You were launching this book in a bad season, and I just came back from the fields, I have had five meetings for the day, I've participated in a graduation ceremony and I rushed back to be here. You almost missed me. So I am sure that my Ministers would be busy out there working, fulfilling other responsibilities. That is the

first point I want to make. The second point is yes, the idea of this book started a long time ago and Arif has been very persistent. I think he spoke with every president starting with Cheddi Jagan and yes, we could not afford the book at that time and you would see although this book is a wonderful book it is pretty expensive too. So we could not afford it at that time. The economy was in a different shape. But even now you may want to ask what has changed? When Arif came to see me about a year ago I said to him that we will do this book but we are only ordering a particular quantity so we have to find other sponsors. This is why I am very pleased that the private sector readily filled that gap. Those who participated willingly and those who we called, they all made a significant contribution to the publication of this book. It is a joint effort and I want to thank all of you for it.

It is an incredible book. I just had it last night and had to sign some 80 copies (autographed copies by President Bharrat Jagdeo were presented to the 40 companies who supported the project, the writers, photographers, the Prime Minister Sam Hinds and other dignitaries) so I just browsed through the book and it's a book that reminds us that we live in a country of breathtaking natural beauty with spectacular heritage sites, unmatched hospitality and a diverse, wonderful, multicultural people. I am very pleased and very proud to live in this country and to be its leader and I am sure that all the people here, when they see this book, it will be heart-warming for them too. I want to thank Arif for this wonderful piece of work.

Arif is internationally renowned and he spoke to you of his struggles that he has had in another country to change the situation there. Although things are better in that country and many others we still have to continue that struggle, because until now racism still stalks the world and wars are fought because of intolerance and because people do not respect and understand each other; their culture, their background and their history and there is too much bigotry in this world and whilst those things remain with us the struggles you have had and the struggles that we all are engaged in will have to continue. But Arif, I am very pleased that you could just come up here and talk about the shape of your foot, normally people would not do that. (Arif Ali, in his presention, referred to his wide feet and offered to take his shoes off, because he did not wear shoes until he was in his teens). But sometimes, today, we are even ashamed of our accent, we want to adopt people's accent because somehow we think it makes us better people and more modern and we would be more accepted. From that perspective, I am glad that you mentioned that. We are a unique people. We are different from other peoples. We have our weaknesses but we have our strengths too and we should all be proud of our upbringing and our past. Maybe not so proud of the bad things and we cannot change them but we have to acknowledge them and move on. I am very proud of you too, because you are Guyanese and you have been serving another country and the world basically.

This book will lure you into a fascinating adventure, one that comes with the discovery of a land rich in history and culture and this book is alive in the quest to surmount the challenges of development. You are not going to see just all the best buildings like in a tourism marketing video. You are going to see the reality of life in Guyana. The shacks and people walking around the streets without shirt and the donkey carts roaming our cities because it is who we are, it is our way of life and the book attempts to portray that. I think this book will open our eyes to the beauty of our country and lead us to appreciate our homeland better, especially for those of us who live here.

I spent Monday, Tuesday and Wednesday in Regions 7 and 8 going up the Pomeroom River and then just branching off into the Mazaruni. The rain was falling and the raindrops were huge and your first instinct is to cover up and then after some time you just allow yourself to be soaked. But this is a feeling of being alive and happy that you're there and you're part of this. It is a feeling that you cannot have on the coast. I was sitting in a guesthouse in Lethum at 5am in the morning with Gerry Gouveia and a few others watching the sun rise over the savannah with the mountains in the background. You feel your heart expand. This is the country that

we live in. You don't get that feeling every day in the hustle and bustle of the city. But I wish more of our people would first of all have an interest and I hope this book will stimulate that interest and then they would have the experience of going out there and being part of this wonderful country. I hope that this book will reawaken in us a sense of nationalism and pride not ignorance and bigotry but a positive nationalism so that we can work together to improve this country. I hope that it will serve to bring our people together because it speaks about our shared heritage, all of us sharing this land together. I hope that it will reinforce these bonds and I hope that someday every child will have the opportunity to see all of the country in its spectacular beauty.

Secondly, I am hoping that this book serves to change our image abroad. This is the first time we are going to have a substantial, substantive piece of work done by a non-politician or one our editors. Often politicians have a partisan view of the world and even when they promote the country they tend to change things to suit the particular outlook. Our newspaper editors also in many ways are more concerned about selling newspapers than presenting a balanced wholesome picture of this country and its beauty. This is the first effort where we have a book that is not about politics and not about making news. This book is just about Guyana and its people. It does not try, as I said before, to polish things up, it shows it in its natural state.

I hope that the book will also expand our effort in creating a huge tourist industry. It is in the fledgling stages, we still have a long way to go but by changing the image of Guyana, by getting people to be familiar with some of the things that we have to offer here, we hope that this will give a big impetus to the tourism drive and tourism is very important in our future. It is part of our effort to diversify our economy. Many of you are aware that the march of globalisation has not been kind to the developing world. Many countries in different parts of Asia, Africa and the Caribbean are faced with severe dislocations because of changes in the world's economic and trading regimes. Changes over which they have very little say and they are not very sure as yet as to what will fill the vacuum created by those changes. Most of us are in this state of turmoil at least in terms of restructuring our economies. We in Guyana, given these concerns think we have a clear vision of where we want to go and essential to that vision is the restructuring of our economy and showing that the traditional industries are internationally competitive and creating a whole new range of industries to add to the stock of wealth of this country and improve income and employment opportunities for our people. The tourism sector is one of the key sectors in this regard. The book also speaks about investment. It speaks in a short way about what we have on offer because we did not want to duplicate the investors' guide, so it mentions the investors' guide and someone can easily go to that website or get a copy of the investors' guide which is much more detailed. It mentions the IPC strategy, the partnership between the government and the private sector. So we hope that if people are more aware of the opportunities here, which this book will help to do, then we may be able to attract the investment in those areas which are critical to the restructuring of our economy because we do not have enough investable resources here in Guyana, although we do have good projects. The source of investment resources is limited and that was because for a long period in Guyana we did not accumulate wealth. We de-accumulated wealth, one of the few countries in this region that did that, and hence the huge foreign debt because the debt was the result of de-accumulation of the wealth and our desire to live at the same standard of living, so we could not sustain that standard of living so we borrowed. And today Arif that is why we are better able to spend a bit more money on tourism. This year we have about GUY$80 million that the government has put into the tourism sector and we are spending a bit more money doing this because our debt servicing has come down from some 94% of revenue to 12% of revenue and we are very thankful to the donors who have supported us. But do not forget it is not through donors' efforts alone that we are here, because in the last 10 years we repaid US$1.1 billion. We repaid more money than we received in development assistance from all the donors combined.

You can see it in some parts of the book, the poverty in some sections of our land. It is through the images that you see this and therefore it will constantly remind us that there is this challenge of overcoming poverty.

More importantly this book speaks about the openness of Guyana, it is a country that still has security challenges, it is still a fledgling democracy but it speaks about the openness of the country, the media, the policies etc and I want to say to you that my Government will forever work at defending those freedoms, the freedoms that we enjoy today. People ask me sometimes why is it that you tolerate all these criticisms, can't you do something about these TV stations, and I say no. We may disagree with what they say but my Government will go down the line of defending their right to say. We may disagree but we will defend their right to say. I think to some extent because a section of the book speaks about the media and about what is happening in media land in Guyana I want to say that that also speaks about the openness of the country. We have a clear vision of where we want to take Guyana. There will be setbacks, problems along the way, nowhere in any part of the world can we have a problem free situation but it is how we rise to these challenges and how we confront and how we can bring to bear all of our resources to confront them that matters. I think this book is not a miracle book, it is not a panacea but it can help to do the things that are important to bring our people together if we allow this message not to remain hidden in the pages of this book, which is kind of expensive, and I am saying that again Arif, but we can make sure that the message gets out to all of our people.

So I want to thank everyone, Arif Ali, his company, the private sector, everyone who has been involved from the government and the private sector. All the contributors to the book for this wonderful piece of work. Arif your name will go down in history as helping to change the perception of this country and it is not that people don't know about Guyana, ask them what they know about Guyana and it is not accurate or it is limited. Now hopefully this book will broaden that vision, that outlook.

I wish now to officially launch the book Arif and hope that a lot of our people will use it productively and that lots of copies sell so you can make lots of money too. And that will encourage you to do more books on Guyana without sponsorship maybe. So this is the book, it is wonderful (President holds up the book). I have seen some images like someone on a bicycle having an innovative way to move plastic bottles or a mother in a canoe with her children, contented rounded babies, just paddling – that is what Guyana is about. I look at this book and I see my country. So please take the opportunity to go through it for yourself and I am sure that you will get the same feeling of pride and joy that I got when I browsed the pages. Thank you very much.

Hansib Book List

1973
Westindians in Great Britain edited by Arif Ali

1974
Westindians in Great Britain (2nd Edition) edited by Arif Ali

1975
Westindians in Britain (3rd Edition) edited by Arif Ali

1979
Westindians in Britain (4th Edition) edited by Arif Ali

1982
Third World Impact (formerly *Westindians in Britain*, 5th Edition) edited by Arif Ali

1983
50 Great West Indian Test Cricketers by Henderson Dalrymple

1984
Third World Impact (6th Edition) edited by Arif Ali

1985
Barrister for the Defence: Trial by Jury and How to Survive It by Rudy Narayan

Rasta & Resistance: From Marcus Garvey to Walter Rodney by Horace Campbell (reprinted 1993, 1997, 2007)

1986
Third World Impact (7th ed.) edited by Arif Ali

1987
Benevolent Neutrality: Indian Government Policy and Labour Migration to British Guiana 1854-1884 by Basdeo Mangru

From Where I Stand by Roy Sawh

India in the Caribbean edited by David Dabydeen & Brinsley Samaroo (reprinted 2006)

My Turn to Bark by Jennifer Muddle

Speeches by Errol Barrow edited by Yussuf Haniff (reprinted 2006)

The Web of Tradition: Uses of Allusion in V. S. Naipaul's Fiction by John Thieme

1988
100 Great West Indian Cricketers: From Challenor to Richards by Bridgette Lawrence with Reg Scarlett

Grass Roots in Verse edited by Arif Ali & Catherine Hogben (Foreword by James Berry)

Antigua & Barbuda: A Little Bit of Paradise edited by Arif Ali

Coolie Odyssey by David Dabydeen (reprinted 2006)

Indo-West Indian Cricket by Frank Birbalsingh & Clem Shiwcharan

Inseparable Humanity: An Anthology of Reflections of Shridath Ramphal edited by Ron Sanders

King of Carnival and Other Stories by Willi Chen (reprinted 2006)

1989
Dominica: Nature Island of the Caribbean edited by Arif Ali

Economics of Adoption of New Agricultural Technology: The Case for the Guyana Rice Subsector by C. Michael Henry

Forbidden Freedom: The Story of British Guiana by Cheddi Jagan

1993
Ethnic Minority Directory edited by Arif Ali

A New System of Slavery: The Export of Indian Labour Overseas, 1830-1920 by Hugh Tinker

1994
Against the Tide by Sarah Olowe

Antigua & Barbuda: A Little Bit of Paradise (2nd Edition) edited by Arif Ali

Grenada: Spice Island of the Caribbean edited by Arif Ali

1994
The Other Middle Passage: Journal of a Voyage from Calcutta to Trinidad, 1858 by Ron Ramdin

Pride of Black British Women by Deborah King

Prospero's Return: Historical Essays on Race, Culture & British Society by Paul B. Rich

Forbidden Freedom: The Story of British Guiana (3rd Edition) by Cheddi Jagan

1995
Bhownaggree: Member of Parliament, 1895-1906 by John R. Hinnells & Omar Ralph

Cheddi Jagan: Selected Speeches, 1992-1994 edited by David Dabydeen

Tomorrow's Africa: Conference Report edited by John Gwynn

1996

Antigua & Barbuda: A Little Bit of Paradise (3rd Edition) edited by Arif Ali

Barbados: Just Beyond Your Imagination edited by Arif Ali

Facing the Challenge: A Report of the First National All-Party Convention of Black, Asian and Ethnic Minority Councillors

Lest We Forget: The Experience of World War II West Indian Ex-Service Personnel by Robert N. Murray

The Norman Manley Memorial Lectures 1984-1995 (in association with The Norman Manley Memorial Lecture Committee)

1997

Cornered Tigers: A History of Pakistan's Test Cricket by Adam Licudi with Wasim Raja

The Empty Sleeve: The Story of the West India Regiments of the British Army by Brian Dyde

The Great Marcus Garvey by Liz Mackie (reprinted 2001, 2008)

India: A Wealth of Diversity edited by Arif Ali

Naoroji, the first Asian MP: A Biography of Dadabhai Naoroji, India's Patriot and Britain's MP by Omar Ralph

Saint Lucia: Simply Beautiful edited by Arif Ali

The State of Black Britain, Volume 1 by Aaron Haynes

The State of Black Britain, Volume 2 by Aaron Haynes

The West on Trial: My Fight for Guyana's Freedom by Cheddi Jagan

Women of Substance: Profiles of Asian Women in the UK by Pushpinder Chowdhry

The Rise of West Indian Cricket: From Colony to Nation by Frank Birbalsingh

1998

Black Pearls: The A-Z of Black Footballers in the English Game edited by Al Hamilton with Rodney Hinds

The USA in South America and Other Essays by Cheddi Jagan edited by David Dabydeen

1999

Antigua & Barbuda: A Little Bit of Paradise (4th Edition) edited by Arif Ali

Cities for the Future edited by Keith Vaz. Prefaced by Prime Minister Tony Blair

Remember Me: Achievements of Mixed Race People, Past and Present by Asher & Martin Hoyles (reprinted 2006)

2000

Trinidad & Tobago: Terrific and Tranquil edited by Arif Ali

2001

Classic Caribbean Cooking (reprinted 2008) by Sharon Atkin

How They Made a Million: The Dyke & Dryden Story by Tony Wade

The Modern Book of Muslim Names by Kash Ali

2002

Antigua Vision, Caribbean Reality: Perspectives of Prime Minister Lester Bryant Bird edited by Ronald Michael Sanders

Black Identity in the 20th Century: Expressions of the US and UK African Diaspora edited by Mark Christian

Moving Voices: Black Performance Poetry by Asher & Martin Hoyles

2003

Anguilla: Tranquillity Wrapped in Blue edited by Arif Ali

Crime in The Caibbean by Ronald Sanders

The War Against Terror and Erosion of Rights by Ronald Sanders

The Art of Garnet Ifill: Glimpses of the Sugar Industry by Brinsley Samaroo

Voice of Change: Selected Speeches of Jennifer M. Smith, Premier of Bermuda edited by Walter H. Roban

2004

75 Years of West Indies Cricket, 1928-2003 by Ray Goble & Keith A. P. Sandiford

The Axe Laid to the Root: The Story of Robert Wedderburn by Martin Hoyles

2004

Bibliography of West Indian Church History compiled by Arthur Dayfoot & Roscoe Pierson

Memories of the 20th Century by Jim Thakoordin

Oliver Tambo Speaks compiled by Adelaide Tambo

2005

Antigua & Barbuda: A Little Bit of Paradise (5th Edition) edited by Arif Ali

Crumbled Small: The Commonwealth Caribbean in World Politics by Ronald Sanders

One People Mayor: A Journey by Sebert Graham & Ian Mulder

Saint Lucia: Simply Beautiful (2nd Ed.) edited by Arif Ali

Tobago: Clean, Green and Serene edited by Arif Ali

Write Black, Write British: From Post Colonial to Black British Literature edited by Kadija Sesay

2006

Guyana edited by Arif Ali

The Undiminished Link: Forty Years and Beyond by Victor Waldron

2007

Barbados: Experience the Authentic Caribbean edited by Arif Ali

Black Routes: Legacy of African Diaspora by Brian A. Belton

A Dream Deferred: Guyanese Identity and the Shadow of Colonialism by Stephen Spencer

Dyslexia from a Cultural Perspective by Asher & Martin Hoyles

India: Definitions and Clarifications by Reginald Massey

Meenachi: Fourth Volume of New Poems by Rajandaye Ramkissoon-Chen

The People's Progressive Party of Guyana, 1950-1992: An Oral History by Frank Birbalsingh

Trinidad & Tobago: Terrific and Tranquil (2nd Edition) edited by Arif Ali

2008

Antigua & Barbuda: A Little Bit of Paradise (6th Edition) edited by Arif Ali

A Black Studies Primer: Heroes and Heroines of the African Diaspora by Keith A. P. Sandiford

Ira Aldridge: Celebrated 19th Century Actor by Martin Hoyles

Guyana (2nd Edition) edited by Arif Ali

Shridath Ramphal: The Commonwealth and the World edited by Richard Bourne

Black Deaths in Police Custody and Human Rights: The Failure of the Stephen Lawrence Inquiry by David Mayberry

Wake People Wake: The Sacred and the Profane by Rawle Winston Titus

Between Two Worlds: The Story of Black British Scientist Alan Goffe by Gaia Goffe & Judith Goffe

Billingsly: The Bear with the Crinkled Ear by E. R. Braithwaite

A History of Theatre in Guyana, 1800-2000 by Frank Thomasson

Short and Sweet: A Collection of Guyanese Stories and Fables by Robert J. Fernandes

A Troubled Dream by Jacques Compton

Beacons of Liberation by Shango Baku

Triumph for UNCLOS: The Guyana-Suriname Maritime Arbitration by Shridath Ramphal

2009

Crossbones and Other Stories by Willi Chen

Singleholic by Katherine Bing

Dominica: Nature Island of the Caribbean (2nd Edition) edited by Arif Ali

Themes in African-Guyanese History edited by Winston F. McGowan, James G. Rose & David A. Granger

The West Indians: Portrait of a People by Jacques Compton

The Balgobin Saga by Petamber Persaud

An Introduction to the Theatre Arts by Jacques Compton

The Boy from Willow Bend by Joanne C. Hillhouse

Sacred Silence by Janet Naidu

2010

From Ranji to Rohan: Cricket and Indian Identity in Colonial Guyana 1890s-1960s by Clem Seecharan

What Being Black Is, and What Being Black Isn't by Jacob Whittingham

Jamaica Absolutely edited by Arif Ali

Growing Out: Black Hair, Black Pride by Barbara Blake Hannah

Goodbye Mango Sergeant: Memories of a Jamaican Trench Town Boy by Keith Walker

Caribbean Publishing in Britain: A Tribute to Arif Ali by Asher & Martin Hoyles

Under Basil Leaves: An Anthology of Poems by Paulette Ramsay

Stories and Recipes From The Egg Lady by Carolyn Ali

Rum, Rivalry & Resistance: Fighting for the Carribbean Spirit by Tony Talburt

Bibliography

Adi, Hakim (1995) *The History of the African and Caribbean Communities in Britain*, Hove: Wayland (revised 2007)

Adi, Hakim & Marika Sherwood (2003) *Pan-African History*, London: Routledge

Alleyne, Brian W. (2002) *Radicals Against Race: Black Activism and Cultural Politics*, Oxford: Berg

Anim-Ado, Joan (ed.) (1998) *Leaves in the Wind: Collected Writings of Beryl Gilroy*, London: Mango Publishing

Baker. Bob & Neil Harvey (1985) *Publishing for People*, London: London Labour Library

Balkaran, Lal (2002) *Dictionary of the Guyanese Amerindians*, Ontario: LBA Publications

BBC Caribbean Service (1959) *Going to Britain?*, London: BBC

Benjamin, Ionie (1995) *The Black Press in Britain*, Stoke-on-Trent: Trentham

Birbalsingh, Frank (1988) *Passion and Exile: Essays in Caribbean Literature*, London: Hansib

Birbalsingh, Frank (ed.) (1989) *Indenture and Exile: The Indo-Caribbean Experience*, Toronto: Tsar

Bryant, Joshua (1824) *Account of an Insurrection of the Negro Slaves in the Colony of Demerara which broke out on the 18th August 1823*, Georgetown: Guiana Chronicle Office

Burnett, D. Graham (2000) *Masters of All They Surveyed*, Chicago: University of Chicago Press

Cameron, Norman Eustace (1929-1934) *The Evolution of the Negro,* Georgetown: 'The Argosy' Company

Cameron, Norman Eustace (1931) *Guianese Poetry 1831-1931*, Georgetown: 'The Argosy' Company

Carew, Jan (1958) *Black Midas*, London: The Camelot Press

Carretta, Vincent (ed.) (1996) *Unchained Voices*, Kentucky: The University Press of Kentucky

Carter, Martin (1954) *Poems of Resistance*, London: Lawrence & Wishart

Carter, Trevor (1986) *Shattering Illusions: West Indians in British Politics*, London: Lawrence & Wishart

Costa, Emilia Viotti da (1994) *Crowns of Glory, Tears of Blood: The Demerara Slave Rebellion of 1823*, Oxford: Oxford University Press

Dabydeen, David & Brinsley Samaroo (eds) (1987) *India in the Caribbean*, London: Hansib

Dabydeen, David (ed.) (1992) *Cheddi Jagan: Selected Speeches 1992-1994*, London: Hansib

Dabydeen, David, John Gilmore & Cecily Jones (eds.) (2007) *The Oxford Companion to Black British History*, Oxford: Oxford University Press

D'Aguiar, Fred (1985) *Mama Dot*, London: Chatto & Windus

Daly, Vere T. (1975) *A Short History of the Guyanese People*, London: Macmillan

Das, Mahadai (1988) *Bones*, Leeds: Peepal Tree Press

Dathorne, O. R. (1975) *Dictionary of Guyanese Folklore*, Georgetown: National History and Arts Council

Donnell, Alison & Sarah Lawson Welsh (eds.) (1996) *The Routledge Reader in Caribbean Literature*, London: Routledge

Donnell, Alison (ed.) (2002) *Companion to Contemporary Black British Culture*, London: Routledge

Edwards, Paul & David Dabydeen (1991) *Black Writers in Britain 1760-1890*, Edinburgh: Edinburgh University Press

Fryer, Peter (1984) *Staying Power: The History of Black People in Britain*, London: Pluto Press

Gilroy, Beryl (1976) *Black Teacher*, London: Cassell

Gilroy, Beryl (1986) *Frangipani House*, Oxford: Heinemann

Gilroy, Beryl (1989) *Boy-Sandwich*, Oxford: Heinemann

Gilroy, Beryl (1994) *Sunlight on Sweet Water*, Leeds: Peepal Tree

Glass, Ruth (1960) *Newcomers: The West Indians in London*, London: Allen & Unwin

Goulbourne, Harry (2002) *Caribbean Transnational Experience*, London: Pluto Press

Grant, Cy (2008) *Rivers of Time*, London: Naked Light

Griffiths, Joan (ed.) (1984) *Caribbean Connections*, London: Commission for Racial Equality

Gundara, Jagdish S. & Ian Duffield (eds.) (1992) *Essays on the History of London's Black Press in the 1930s & 1940s*, Aldershot: Avebury

Harris, Wilson (1967) *Tradition the Writer and Society,* London: New Beacon

Heath, Roy (1990) *Shadows Round the Moon: Caribbean Memoirs,* London: Collins

Hemming, John (1978) *The Search for El Dorado*, London: Michael Joseph

Hinds, Donald (1966) *Journey to an Illusion: The West Indian in Britain*, London: Heinemann

Hintzen, Percy (1994) *'The Colonial Foundations of Race Relations and Ethno-Politics in Guyana'*, History Gazette, Number 65, Georgetown: Free Press

Hooker, J. R. (1975) *Henry Sylvester Williams: Imperial Pan-Africanist*, London: Rex Collings

Hoyles, Martin (2004) *The Axe Laid to the Root: The Story of Robert Wedderburn*, London: Hansib

Innes, Catherine Lynette (2002) *A History of Black and Asian Writing in Britain, 1700-2000*, Cambridge: CUP

Jagan, Cheddi (1966) *The West on Trial: My Fight for Guyana's Freedom*, London: Michael Joseph (Hansib 1997)

James, C. L. R. (1936) *Minty Alley*, London: Secker & Warburg

James, Winston & Clive Harris (eds.) (1993) *Inside Babylon: The Caribbean Diaspora in Britain,* London: Verso

Jenkins, Edward (1871) *The Coolie: His Rights and Wrongs*, London: Strahan & Co.

Johnson, Buzz (1985) *'I Think of My Mother': Notes on the Life and Times of Claudia Jones*, London: Karia Press

Johnson, Christopher (2009) *British Caribbean Enterprises: A Century of Challenges and Successes*, London: Johnson

Kanhai, Cyril (1969) *My New Guyana,* Kitty, Guyana: The Author

Khalideen, Rosetta (1979) *Leguan: A Collection of Poems*, East Coast Demerara: Khalideen

King, Kenneth (ed.) (1973) *Ras Makonnen: Pan-Africanism from Within*, London: OUP

Kramer, Ann (2006) *Many Rivers to Cross: The History of the Caribbean Contribution to the NHS*, London: Sugar Media Limited

Lamming, George (1953) *In the Castle of My Skin*, London: Michael Joseph

Laurence, K. O. (1994) *A Question of Labour: Indentured Immigration into Trinidad and British Guiana 1875- 1917*, Kingston: Ian Randle

Lewis, Rupert (1987) *Marcus Garvey: Anti-Colonial Champion*, London: Karia Press

Lovelace, Earl (1979) *The Dragon Can't Dance*, London: Andre Deutsch

Macdonald, Roderick J. (1976) *The Keys: The Official Organ of the League of Coloured Peoples*, New York: Kraus-Thomson

McDonald, Ian (1983) *Selected Poems*, Georgetown: The Labour Advocate

McDonald, Ian (1988) *Mercy Ward*, Cornwall; Peterloo Poets

Mangru, Basdeo (1987) *Benevolent Neutrality*, London: Hansib

Mangru, Basdeo (1996) *A History of East Indian Resistance on the Guyanese Sugar Estates 1869-1948*, New York: Edwin Mellen Press

Mangru, Basdeo (2000) *Indians in Guyana*, Chicago: Adams Press

Mathurin, Owen Charles (1976) *Henry Sylvester Williams and the Origins of the Pan-African Movement, 1869-1911*, Wesport: Greenwood Press

Matthews, Marc (1987) Guyana My Altar, London: Karnak House

Mittelholzer, Edgar (1941) *Corentyne Thunder*, London: Eyre & Spottiswoode

Mittelholzer, Edgar (1963) *A Swarthy Boy*, London: Putnam

Morrison, Lionel (2007) *A Century of Black Journalism in Britain*, London: Truebay

Owusu, Kwesi (ed.) (2000) *Black British Culture & Society*, London: Routledge

Padmore, George (1956) *Pan-Africanisn or Communism?*, London: Dennis Dobson

Patterson, Sheila (1963) *Dark Strangers*, London: Tavistock Publications

Peach, Ceri (1968) *West Indian Migration to Britain*, London: Oxford University Press

Pearson, David (1981) *Race, Class and Political Activism: A Study of West Indians in Britain*, Farnborough: Gower

Phillips, Evan (1974) *A Voice From The Trees*, Guyana: Phillips

Prasad, Krishna (1978) *Flames of Freedom*, Wales, Guyana: The Author

Ramdin, Ron (1987) *The Making of the Black Working Class in Britain*, Aldershot: Gower

Ramdin, Ron (1999) *Reimaging Britain: Five Hundred Years of Black and Asian History*, London: Pluto Press

Rice, Alan (2003) *Radical Narratives of the Black Atlantic*, London: Continuum

Rodney, Walter (1981) *A History of the Guyanese Working People, 1881-1905*, London: Heinemann

Rodway, James & James H. Stark (1895) *Stark's Guide-Book and History of British Guiana,* Boston: James H. Stark

Rohlehr, Gordon (2007) *Transgression, Transition, Transformation*, San Juan: Lexicon Trinidad

Sadeek, Sheik (1980) *Wind-Swept and Other Stories*, Georgetown: Sadeek

Sancho, T. Anson (1966) *Highlights of Guyanese History*, Georgetown: An Independence Publication

Sancho, T. Anson (1970) *The Ballad of 1763: The Story of Cuffy's Rebellion Narrated in Verse*, Georgetown

Sawh, Roy (1987) *From Where I Stand*, London: Hansib

Schwarz, Bill (ed.) (2003) *West Indian Intellectuals in Britain,* Manchester*:* Manchester University Press

Scobie, Edward (1972) *Black Britannia: A History of Blacks in Britain*, Chicago: Johnson

Searwar, Lloyd, Ian McDonald, Laxhmie Kallicharan & Joel Benjamin (eds.) (1998) *They Came in Ships: An Anthology of Indo-Guyanese Prose and Poetry*, Leeds: Peepal Tree

Seecharan, Clem (1993) *India and the Shaping of the Indo-Guyanese Imagination 1890s-1920s*, Leeds: Peepal Tree Press

Seecharan, Clem (1997) *'Tiger in the Stars': The Anatomy of Indian Achievement in British Guiana 1919-29*, London: Macmillan

Seecharan, Clem (1999) *Bechu: 'Bound Coolie' Radical in British Guiana 1894-1901*, Kingston: University of West Indies Press

Seecharan, Clem (2001) *Joseph Ruhomon's India*, Kingston: University of the West Indies Press

Seecharan, Clem (2005) *Sweetening Bitter Sugar: Jock Campbell, the Booker Reformer in British Guiana 1934-1966*, Kingston: Ian Randle

Seecharan, Clem (2006) *Muscular Learning*, Kingston: Ian Randle

Selvon, Samuel (1956) *The Lonely Londoners*, London: Alan Wingate

Seymour, A. J. (ed.) (1961) *Themes of Song: An Anthology of Guianese Poetry*, Georgetown

Seymour, A. J. (1980) *The Making of Guyanese Literature*, Georgetown, Guyana

Seymour, A. J. (ed.) (1980) *A Treasury of Guyanese Poetry*, Guyana: GTM

Sherwood, Marika (1999) *Claudia Jones: A Life in Exile*, London: Lawrence & Wishart

Shinebourne, Janice (1986) *Timepiece*, Leeds: Peepal Tree Press

Spencer, Stephen (2007) *A Dream Deferred*, London: Hansib

Thompson, Alvin O. (1987) *Colonialism and Underdevelopment in Guyana 1580-1803*, Bridgetown: Carib Research & Publications

Thompson, Alvin O. (1997) *The Haunting Past*, Kingston: Ian Randle

Thompson, Alvin O. (2002) *A Documentary History of Slavery in Berbice*, Georgetown: Free Press

Thompson, Clarence C. (1973) *Portrait of a People*, London: Free University for Black Studies

Tinker, Hugh (1974) *A New System of Slavery*, London: Oxford University Press (Hansib 1993)

Van Sertima, Ivan (1976) *They Came Before Columbus*, New York: Random House

Wade, Tony (2007) *The Adventures of an Economic Migrant*, Kingston, Jamaica: Ian Randle

Walmsley, Anne (ed.) (1990) *Guyana Dreaming: The Art of Aubrey Williams*, Sydney: Dangaroo Press

Walmsley, Anne (1992) *The Caribbean Artists Movement 1966-1972*, London: New Beacon

Wambu, Onyekachi (ed.) (1998) *Empire Windrush: Fifty Years of Writing About Black Britain*, London: Gollancz

Webber, A. R. F. (1931) *Centenary History and Handbook of British Guiana*, British Guiana: The Argosy

Williams, Denis (1995) *Pages in Guyanese Prehistory*, Georgetown: Walter Roth Museum of Anthropology

Williams, Denis (2003) *Prehistoric Guyana*, Kingston: Ian Randle

Williams, Milton Vishnu (1986) *Years of Fighting Exile*, Leeds: Peepal Tree Press

Yansen. C. A. (1993) *Random Remarks on Creolese*, London: Sonja Jansen